THE ESSENTIAL GUIDE TO
GEOMETRY

유하림(Harim Yoo) 지음

The Essential Guide to Geometry

초판 1쇄 발행 2020년 6월 17일
개정 1쇄 발행 2025년 1월 17일

저자 유하림
발행인 최영민
발행처 피앤피북
주소 경기도 파주시 신촌로 16
전화 031-8071-0088
팩스 031-942-8688
전자우편 hermonh@naver.com
출판등록 2015년 3월 27일
등록번호 제406-2015-31호

ISBN 979-11-94085-35-5 (53410)

- 헤르몬하우스는 피앤피북의 임프린트 출판사입니다.
- 이 책의 어느 부분도 저작권자나 발행인의 승인 없이 무단 복제하여 이용할 수 없습니다.
- 정가는 뒤 표지에 있습니다.

❖ 저자직강 인터넷 강의는 SAT, AP No.1 인터넷 강의 사이트인 마스터프랩 (www.masterprep.net) 에서 보실 수 있습니다.

압구정 현장에서 믿고 찾는 유하림 커리큘럼
Essential Math Series #3

THE ESSENTIAL GUIDE TO
GEOMETRY

유하림(Harim Yoo) 지음

Geometry 기본 교과 개념부터 응용까지
유학 준비생을 위한 Geometry 핵심 개념편

Preface

To. 학부모님과 학생들께

압구정 현장 강의를 통해 6학년부터 12학년까지 가르치며, 이 교재를 출간한 지 어느덧 4년의 세월이 지났습니다. 학부모님과 학생들의 사랑을 힘입어, 이 교재를 개편하는 시점까지 올 수 있었습니다. 유하림 커리큘럼의 시작으로 이 교재를 출판하고 난 이후, Geometry 교재에 대한 피드백을 듣고, 이에 맞춰 수정하여, 개정판을 출간하게 되었습니다.

Geometry를 처음 배우는 학생들이 매우 흥미롭게 배울 수 있도록, 현장에서 검증된 내용 위주로 작성하였기 때문에, 한국인 입맛에 딱 맞춘 교재라고 볼 수 있습니다. 시작하려는 학생에게 너무 어렵지도 않게, 그렇다고 매우 기본적인 내용만 들어간 것은 아니기 때문에, 이 해당 교재를 통해, 인터넷 강의를 듣거나, 제 현장 강의를 듣는 학생들에게는 아주 손쉽게 Geometry의 벽을 넘길 수 있다고 자신합니다.

이 교재를 출간할 수 있도록 물심양면으로 힘써 주신 마스터프렙 권주근 대표님께 감사합니다. 그리고 이 교재를 실제로 출판할 수 있도록 도와주신 피앤피북 대표님께도 감사합니다. 언제나 든든한 지원군인 제 아내, 딸, 그리고 부모님께도 항상 감사합니다. 마지막으로 제 삶에 이러한 기회를 주신 하나님께 감사합니다. 앞으로도 더 좋은 교재를 만들어 견고하고 튼튼한 유하림 커리큘럼을 완성하도록 하겠습니다.

2024년 겨울
유하림

저자 소개

유하림(Harim Yoo)

미국 Northwestern University,
B.A. in Mathematics and Economics
(노스웨스턴 대학교 수학과/경제학과 졸업)

마스터프렙 수학영역 대표강사
압구정 현장강의 ReachPrep 원장

[저 서]
몰입공부
The Essential Guide to Prealgebra
The Essential Guide to Algebra 1
The Essential Guide to Geometry
The Essential Guide to Algebra 2
The Essential Guide to Precalculus
The Essential Workbook for SAT Math Level 2
The Essential Guide to SAT Math Level 2
The Essential Guide to IGCSE : Addmath
The Essential Guide to Competition Math (Fundamentals)
The Essential Guide to Number Theory (Competition Math)
The Essential Guide to Counting and Probability (Competition Math)

이 책의 특징

Geometry의 핵심을 단기간에 공부할 수 있도록 정리해 둔 Essential Guide가 되도록 희망하면서, 이 교재를 집필하였습니다. 특히, 미국 명문 Junior Boarding School 및 Boarding School을 진학하고, 성공적으로 적응하기 위해 필요한 내용이 무엇일지 고민하였고, 8학년(예비 9학년)에게 제일 필요한 Geometry 수학 교재로써 필요한 것이 무엇인지 고민하면서 다년간 작업한 교재입니다.

이 책을 통해, 혼자서 고민하고 공부할 학생들과 마스터프렙 인강을 통해 공부할 학생들, 그리고 현장 강의를 통해 저와 함께 공부할 학생들을 위해, 기본에 가장 충실한 교재를 집필하고자 노력했습니다. 기존에 공부해 왔던 120 예제뿐 아니라 추가적으로 Skill Practice와 Example이 추가되었습니다. 학생의 눈높이에 맞춘 책이라는 것을 자신 있게 말씀드립니다.

2nd 탄탄한 내신 관리를 위한 책

The Essential Guide to Geometry의 경우, 짧은 기간에 폭발적으로 공부할 수 있는 교재입니다. 현대 사회에 가장 필요한 교재 형태에 맞춘 교재라고 볼 수 있습니다. 단기간에 Geometry를 복습하고자 하는 학생뿐만 아니라, 선행하고자 하는 학생 모두에게 도움이 되고자 작성한 교재입니다. 내신 만점을 받기 위한 예제들로부터 증명 문제를 주로 다루기 때문에, 엄선된 120개의 예제와 추가된 Examples 그리고 Skill Practice를 토대로 기하학적으로 사고하는 방법을 배울 수 있도록 저술하였습니다.

3rd 유학생을 위한 단 한 권의 책

미국수학을 정말 미국수학 답게 가르치기 위해 열심히 공부하고 연구하고, 앞으로도 그러할 것입니다. 저를 현장에서 만나 본 학생 및 학부모들은 모두 아시겠지만, 저는 이 분야를 진심으로 즐거워하고 재밌어하는 강사 중 한 명입니다. 여러분이 지금 보는 이 책은 제 현재 노력의 최선의 산실이며, 앞으로도 그러할 것입니다. 이 책을 통해 수학을 두려워하지 않고, 문제 해결을 즐거워하며, 이른 나이에 수학에 대한 열정을 꽃피우길 기대합니다.

CONTENTS

Preface   4
저자 소개   5
이 책의 특징   6

Topic 1 Basic Elements of Geometry 11
1.1 Points, Lines, and Planes.. 12
1.2 Line, Segment, and Ray 15
1.3 Coordinate Plane... 18
1.4 Angle and Its Measure... 21
1.5 Relationship between Geometric Objects 25

Topic 2 Mathematical Reasoning 39
2.1 Induction and Deduction.. 40
2.2 Algebraic Proof and Geometric Proof 45
2.3 Basic Postulates for Segments and Angles...................... 46

Topic 3 Parallel and Perpendicular Lines.......................... 59
3.1 Parallel Lines and Transversal 60
3.2 Distance Formula Revisited 63

Topic 4 Congruent Triangles.. 75
4.1 Basic Classification of Triangles...................................... 76
4.2 Congruent Triangles 78
4.3 Congruence Postulates 80
4.4 Finding Congruent Triangles in Isosceles Triangle 81

Topic 5 Triangle Properties.. 95
5.1 Angle Bisector Theorem... 96
5.2 Points of Concurrency 98
5.3 Properties of Right Triangle 101
5.4 Triangular Inequality.. 102

Topic 6 Similar Triangles 115
6.1 Similar Triangles.. 116

Topic 7 Quadrilateral 129
7.1 Quadrilateral and Trapezoid 130
7.2 Parallelogram, Rhombus, Rectangle and Square 133

Topic 8 Polygons 149
8.1 Introduction to Polygon 150
8.2 Angle Chasing 151
8.3 Area of Polygon (Hexagon or Octagon) 153
8.4 Diagonals of Polygons 156

Topic 9 Circles... 163
9.1 Terminology 164
9.2 Arcs, Angles and Chords 165

Topic 10 Transformation 183
10.1 Translation and Rotation 184
10.2 Reflection and Dilation 187

Topic 11 Solid Figures.. 197
11.1 Polyhedron and Solids of Revolution........................... 198
11.2 Surface Area... 202
11.3 Volume 206

Topic 12 Trigonometric Ratio 215
12.1 Basic Ratio... 216

Solution to 120 Walk-Through Exercises 225

Topic 1
Basic Elements of Geometry

1.1 Points, Lines, and Planes 12
1.2 Line, Segment, and Ray 15
1.3 Coordinate Plane 18
1.4 Angle and Its Measure 21
1.5 Relationship between Geometric Objects 25

1.1 Points, Lines, and Planes

Conventionally, we say there are three geometric objects for basic elements of geometry. In "Elements" written by Euclid, point, line and plane are defined in the following form.

- **Point**: A point is an exact location in space that has no size, dimension, or shape. It is often represented by a dot and labeled with a capital letter.

- **Line**: A line is a straight one-dimensional figure that extends infinitely in both directions. It has length but no width and is determined by at least two points.

- **Plane**: A plane is a flat, two-dimensional surface that extends infinitely in all directions. It has length and width but no thickness and is defined by three non-collinear points.

In this book, this is how they are defined.

(1) Point is a dot that has no dimension.

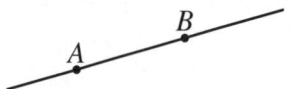

(2) Line is a straight line consisting of infinitely many points.

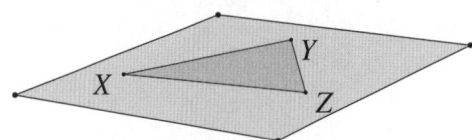

(3) Plane looks like a flat sheet of surface that does not end, containing infinitely many points.

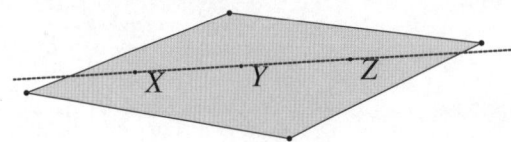

Two different points form a unique line. How about three distinct points? They usually do not form a unique line. If three points are aligned in a single line, we say the three points are *collinear*. Three points that are not collinear form a plane. So, we say they are coplanar. Coplanar points are points on single plane.

Example 1

Fill the blanks.

(1) The basic elements of Geometry are ____, ____, and ____.

(2) A line consists of _____ many points, and its shape is _____.

(3) Out of surfaces, a _____ surface is a plane.

Example 2

Is it common to have three collinear points in a plane?

Example 3

What is the length of a dot A?

Example 4

If points X, Y and Z are placed in the same plane such that the line $\overline{XY}$ contains Z, is it true that X, Y and Z are collinear?

Example 5

For three non-collinear points A, B, and C, count the total number of lines containing at least two points.

Here is the short-solution to the examples covered in the previous page.

Example 1. The following words are answers to example 1.
(1) point, line, plane.
(2) infinitely, straight.
(3) flat

Example 2. No. Normally, if you throw three balls in the field, it would not be collinear. Three balls lying on the field in a straight line are extremely rare. Hence, it is worthwhile to study this special case.

Example 3. The length of a dot A, were to be computed, must be 0.

Example 4. Yes. If the line $\overline{XY}$ contains Z, it means X, Y and Z are on the same line. This implies that X, Y and Z are collinear.

Example 5. We can count this by hand. First, two different points form a unique line. Notice that the line $\overline{AB}$ must be exactly the same line $\overline{BA}$. In other words, we choose two letters from the three letters, i.e.,

$$\overleftrightarrow{AB}, \overleftrightarrow{AC}, \overleftrightarrow{BC}$$

HISTORICAL FACT

The fundamental concepts of point, line, and plane have their roots in ancient Greek mathematics, particularly in the work of Euclid around 300 BCE. In his seminal text "Elements," Euclid defined a point as that which has no part, a line as breadthless length, and a plane as a flat surface extending infinitely in all directions. These seemingly simple definitions laid the groundwork for what we now know as Euclidean geometry.

Euclids approach was revolutionary because it provided a systematic and logical framework for understanding the space around us. His axiomatic method, where complex theorems were derived from a small set of simple postulates, became the standard for mathematical proofs for centuries.

Despite the development of non-Euclidean geometries in the 19th century, Euclid's definitions remain foundational in mathematics education and are crucial for fields such as architecture, engineering, and physics. His work has influenced not just mathematics but also the way we conceptualize and interact with the physical world.

Geometry teaches students how to think abstractly and apply mathematical concepts to real-world situations, such as in engineering, architecture, and computer graphics. It also provides a basis for more advanced topics like calculus and physics. By mastering these fundamental concepts, students build a strong foundation for STEM fields and learn to approach complex problems with clarity and precision.

1.2 Line, Segment, and Ray

1. Line AB : $\overleftrightarrow{AB}$ or $\overleftrightarrow{BA}$.

2. Ray AB : $\overrightarrow{AB}$, which is a unique expression for the given geometric object.

3. Segment AB : $\overline{AB}$ or $\overline{BA}$.

Segment consists of two endpoints. Given two endpoints A and B, a line segment AB is $\overline{AB}$. Ray consists of one endpoint and all the other points on a consistent direction from the endpoint. Given two points, A and B, where A is the endpoint, a ray AB is $\overrightarrow{AB}$. If A, B, C are collinear in the written order, then $\overrightarrow{BA}$ and $\overrightarrow{BC}$ are opposite rays. Similar to collinear points and coplanar points, "lines, rays, or segments" could be coplanar or collinear(usually for rays and segments).

Line segments with same length are "congruent segments." If lengths are equal, then segments must be congruent. If $|\overline{AB}| = |\overline{CD}|$, then $\overline{AB} \cong \overline{CD}$. Usually, in Geometry textbooks, if $AB = CD$, then $\overline{AB} \cong \overline{CD}$. The former represents equal lengths, while the latter represents congruent sides.

How do we construct a congruent segment? In order to copy a segment, we use the following construction rule.

1. Draw any segment $\overline{XY}$. Draw a line and a point on the line. Label it U.

2. Place the compass at the point X and adjust the compass setting so that the pen is at the point Y.

3. Using the same setting, put the compass point at U and draw an arc around the line so that it intersects the line. Label it V. Then, we have $\overline{XY} \cong \overline{UV}$.

$$\overline{AB} \cong \overline{CD} \text{ (segment congruence)}$$

$$AB = CD \text{ (length equality)}$$

Let's talk about special point(s) and line(s). First, what is a midpoint? A *midpoint* of a segment is a point that divides the segment into half. This point is unique for any given segment.

For any segment $\overline{AB}$, if the coordinate of A is a, and the coordinate of B is b, then the coordinate of the midpoint of AB is equal to $\dfrac{a+b}{2}$. Have a look at the following figure.

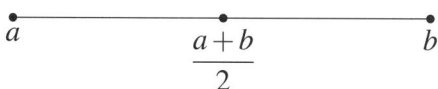

A *bisector* of a line segment is a point, ray, line, or line segment that goes trough the midpoint. Here, a line cannot be bisected because it extends infinitely into opposite directions.

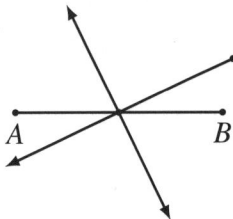

In order to bisect a segment, we use the following construction rule.

1. Draw any segment $\overline{XY}$. Place the compass at point X and adjust it with its length longer than half of XY. Draw arcs above and below $\overline{XY}$.

2. Repeat the same process with the same compass setting at point Y. Label the intersection points as U and V.

3. Draw $\overline{UV}$, a bisector of $\overline{XY}$.

Example 6

If $\overline{AB}$ and $\overline{CD}$ are congruent, and $AB = 4$ and $CD = 3x - 5$, find the value of x.

Example 7

If $\overline{MN}$ and $\overline{RS}$ are congruent, and $MN = 2x - 15$ and $RS = 5 - 3x$, there is a problem associated to the algebraic solution. What is it?

Example 8

On a real line, if X has the coordinate of -3 and Y has the coordinate of 8, find the midpoint of $\overline{XY}$.

Here is the short-solution to the examples covered in the previous page.

Example 6. Since congruent segments have equal lengths, we get $AB = CD$. Therefore, $4 = 3x - 5$, so $3x = 9$. Hence, $x = 3$.

Example 7. If we let $MN = RS$, then

$$2x - 15 = 5 - 3x$$
$$5x = 20$$
$$x = 4$$

However, if we substitute $x = 4$, then $MN = 2(4) - 15 = -7 < 0$. This leads to a contradiction because length must be at non-negative.

Example 8. Let the coordinate of the midpoint be a. Then, $a - (-3) = 8 - a$, since it is the distance from a midpoint to each of the points must be equal to one another. Rearranging variables and constants, we get $2a = 5$. Therefore, $a = 5/2 = 2.5$.

HISTORICAL FACT

The concepts of midpoint and bisector have their origins in ancient Greek mathematics, where mathematicians such as Euclid and Archimedes made significant contributions. The midpoint, which divides a line segment into two equal parts, was essential in geometric constructions and proofs. Euclids work in his "Elements" around 300 BCE laid the groundwork for using midpoints in various propositions and theorems.

The bisector, which can be a line, ray, or plane that divides an angle or segment into two equal parts, was also crucial for developing constructions such as the perpendicular bisector and angle bisector. These constructions were used by the Greeks to solve problems like constructing perpendicular lines or finding the center of a circle.

In the 17th century, René Descartes further formalized the use of midpoints and bisectors in the Cartesian coordinate system, making these concepts more accessible and applicable to algebraic methods. However, it was in the 19th century that these geometric ideas were expanded significantly. Mathematicians like Karl von Staudt and Felix Klein integrated projective geometry and group theory with classical concepts like midpoints and bisectors. This integration allowed for a deeper understanding of geometric properties and symmetries, providing a bridge between classical Euclidean geometry and more abstract mathematical theories.

Today, midpoints and bisectors are fundamental in fields like geometry, trigonometry, and even computer science, where they are used in algorithms for graphics and game development. Understanding these concepts is crucial for developing a strong foundation in mathematical reasoning and problem-solving.

1.3 Coordinate Plane

Coordinate plane, in plane geometry, is usually a two-dimensional plane with an ordered pair.

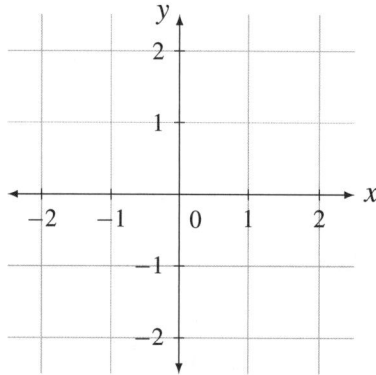

As you can see from the diagram above, when we plot any point, we use the coordinate system. For instance, suppose you are given with (a,b). Then, we plot the point by moving a units horizontally from the origin and b units vertically from the origin to plot the point. Here, a is known as *abscissa* and y is *ordinate*. Specifically, suppose you have a point $(1,2)$. We start from the Origin, which is the intersection point of the x-axis (the thick horizontal line) and the y-axis (the thick vertical line). Then, we move 1 unit right and 2 unit up from $(0,0)$.

The following formulas are both midpoint formula and distance formula in two dimensional cases. In later chapters(or sections), you would see why they are true.

1. Midpoint formula : given two points $A(a,b)$ and $B(c,d)$, the midpoint of $\overline{AB}$ is
$$\left(\frac{a+c}{2}, \frac{b+d}{2}\right)$$

2. Distance formula : given two points $A(a,b)$ and $B(c,d)$, the distance between A and B is
$$\sqrt{(a-c)^2 + (b-d)^2}$$

When we get the coordinates, we can simply compute in terms of one dimensional case. The bottom colorbox illustrates historical backgrounds on quadrants.

HISTORICAL FACT

The concept of quadrants in the coordinate plane divides the plane into four regions, named I, II, III, and IV, based on the signs of x and y coordinates. This system, established by René Descartes in the 17th century, helps in identifying the position of points and understanding the behavior of functions in different regions.

Example 9

If $A(1,4)$ and $B(3,-2)$ are given points on the coordinate plane, find the midpoint M of $\overline{AB}$.

Example 10

How much does it move from $(1,5)$ to $(5,10)$? Express your answer as $<a,b>$ where a is the amount of move in the x-direction and b the amount of move in the y-direction.

Example 11

Determine the area formed by the triangle $(0,0)$, $(2,3)$ and $(4,0)$.

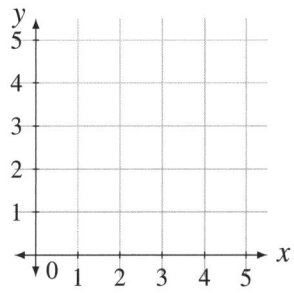

Example 12

Determine the area formed by the triangle $(0,0)$, $(1,3)$ and $(4,1)$.

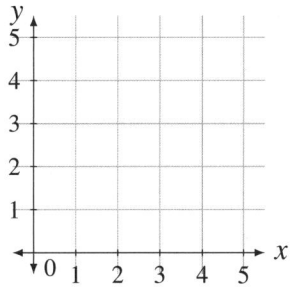

Here is the short solution to the examples covered in the previous page.

Example 9. According to the midpoint formula, we get $\left(\dfrac{1+3}{2}, \dfrac{4+(-2)}{2}\right) = (2,1)$.

Example 10. From 1 to 5, there is an increase of 4. Likewise, from 5 to 10, there is an increase of 5. Hence, we conclude that $<a,b> = <4,5>$.

Example 11. Notice that two points $(0,0)$ and $(4,0)$ are horizontal. Hence, we use the conventional area method. The base has the length of 4, and the height is 3. Thus, the area is $\dfrac{1}{2} \times 4 \times 3 = 6$.

Example 12. Draw vertical and horizontal lines passing through $(0,0)$, $(1,3)$ and $(4,1)$. The area of a triangle is 5.5 by taking three right triangles away from the rectangle.

HISTORICAL FACT

The concept of the coordinate plane, also known as the Cartesian plane, originated in the 17th century with the French mathematician René Descartes. Descartes introduced a revolutionary way to represent geometric shapes and algebraic equations using a two-dimensional grid, where points are defined by pairs of numbers (x,y). This breakthrough allowed for the unification of algebra and geometry, a significant development that laid the groundwork for analytical geometry.

Before Descartes, geometry was mostly studied in a purely geometric sense, as seen in Euclids "Elements," which focused on constructions using only a compass and straightedge. Descartes' method enabled mathematicians to represent geometric figures algebraically and solve geometric problems with equations. This innovation opened up new avenues for solving complex problems in mathematics and the physical sciences.

In the 19th century, the coordinate plane concept was further developed with the introduction of the complex plane by Carl Friedrich Gauss, which extended the idea of coordinates to complex numbers. This development greatly enhanced the mathematical toolkit for analyzing functions and transformations in the complex domain. Complex plane will be covered in Precalculus in detail.

Today, the coordinate plane is a fundamental concept in mathematics education, used extensively in fields such as physics, engineering, computer graphics, and data visualization. It serves as the basis for understanding more advanced topics like calculus, vector spaces, and multi-dimensional geometry. The coordinate plane has become an essential tool for translating abstract mathematical ideas into practical applications in the real world.

1.4 Angle and Its Measure

Angle is the amount of rotation from the given ray to another given ray, both of which start from the common endpoint.

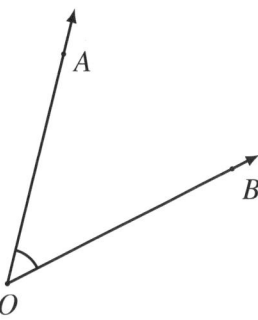

The representation of angle is given by ∠AOB, ∠BOA, and ∠O. The rays(segments) are *sides* and the common endpoint is *vertex*. The region enclosed by rays is called *the interior of the angle*, while the other region is called *the exterior of the angle*.

The following list is the classification of angles by its measure. Let A be an angle.

1. Acute angle : $0° < m\angle A < 90°$.
2. Right angle : $90° = m\angle A$.
3. Obtuse angle : $90° < m\angle A < 180°$.
4. Straight angle : $180° = m\angle A$.
5. Reflex angle : $180° < m\angle A$.

Similar to congruent segments, angles are *congruent* if and only if they have the same measure. If $m\angle ABC = m\angle DEF$, then $\angle ABC \cong \angle DEF$.

Given two distinct lines on a plane, they may intersect at a point. This point is called *the point of intersection*. Look at the following figure.

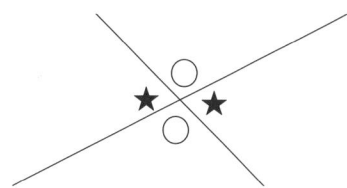

In the figure, stars look at each other, as circles do. These angles are called *vertical angles*. Vertical angles are always congruent. This book calls it "Vertical Angle Postulate," or VAP (as an abbreviation).

Vertical Angle Postulate
When two lines intersect, the opposite (or vertical) angles formed are congruent.

In order to copy an angle, we use the following construction method.

1. Draw an angle X. Use a straightedge to draw a different ray on the same sheet of paper. Label it U.

2. Place the tip of the compass at point X and draw somewhat large arc that intersects both sides. Label it A and B.

3. Use the same compass setting to draw the arc by placing the tip of the compass at U. Label the intersection point V.

4. Place the point of the compass on A and adjust so that the pencil tip is on B.

5. Use the same compass setting, place the compass at V and draw an arc to intersect the original large arc. Label the point of intersection W.

6. Use a straightedge to draw $\overrightarrow{UW}$.

Next, a *bisector of an angle* is a ray whose endpoint is the vertex of the angle, and that divides the angle into two congruent angles.

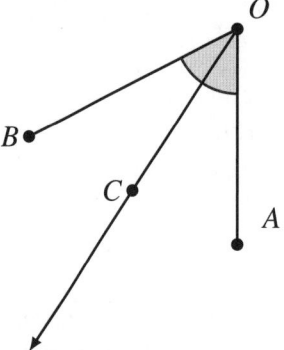

If the given angle is a straight angle, a bisector of the angle forms a right angle. Here, perpendicular lines are the lines to form right angles.

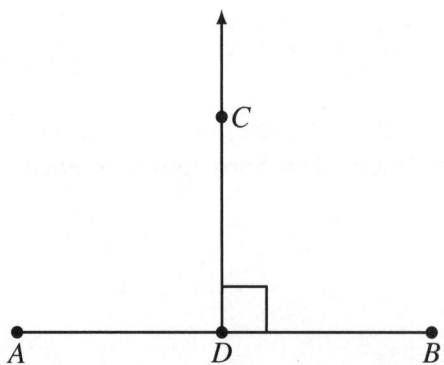

22   The Essential Guide to Geometry

The distance from a point C, in this case, to a line segment $\overline{AB}$ is the length of the perpendicular from the point to the segment. The point of intersection(here, D) is called the foot of the perpendicular. In this case, the distance is CD.

The following procedures show how to construct an angle bisector.

1. Draw an angle and label the vertex X. Put the compass at X and draw a large arc around the angle. Label the intersection points Y and Z.

2. Use the compass, place it at point Y, and draw an arc in the interior of the angle.

3. Use the same compass setting, place it at point Z and draw an arc in the interior of the angle.

4. Label the point of intersection W. Draw $\overrightarrow{XW}$. This is the angle bisector.

Finally, let's go over all angle pair relationships.

(1) Complementary Angle Pairs : two angles are *complementary* if the sum of the angles forms 90° in their measures.

(2) Supplementary Angle Pairs : two angles are *supplementary* if the sum of the angles forms 180° in their measures.

(3) Adjacent Angle Pairs : two angles are *adjacent* if they share *a vertex and a side*, but no interior point.

(4) Non-adjacent Angle Pairs : two angles are *nonadjacent* if they are not adjacent.

(5) Linear Pair : a pair of adjacent angles whose non-common sides are opposite rays.

Example 13

If $\angle A$ and $\angle B$ are congruent, where $m\angle A = (45-x)°$ and $m\angle B = (2x-15)°$, find x.

Example 14

If $\angle A$ and $\angle B$ are supplementary angles, and $m\angle A = 3x - 10°$ and $m\angle B = 20° - x$, find the value of x.

Here is the short solution to the examples covered in the previous page.

Example 13. Two congruent angles have same measures. Therefore, we solve

$$45 - x = 2x - 15$$
$$60 = 3x$$
$$20 = x$$

Example 14. Since A and B are supplementary, we get $3x - 10° + 20° - x = 180°$. Hence, $2x + 10° = 180°$, so $2x = 170°$, so we get $85°$.

HISTORICAL FACT

The concept of the angle bisector has been studied since ancient times, with its roots tracing back to Greek mathematicians such as Euclid. In his work "Elements," Euclid outlined the angle bisector as a line or segment that divides an angle into two equal parts. This property was essential in classical geometric constructions, such as constructing a triangle's incenter, which is the point where all three angle bisectors intersect. The incenter is the center of the inscribed circle of the triangle, showcasing the significance of angle bisectors in geometric theory and application.

In the Islamic Golden Age, mathematicians like Al-Khwarizmi and Al-Kashi further explored angle bisectors, developing more sophisticated methods for geometric constructions and solving equations. The study of angle bisectors continued to evolve with the development of trigonometry and algebra, as these fields provided new tools for analyzing and applying geometric principles.

In the 19th century, the study of angle bisectors was expanded by mathematicians such as Jakob Steiner, who explored their properties in relation to projective geometry. This allowed for a deeper understanding of the relationships between angles, circles, and other geometric figures.

Today, the angle bisector theorem is a fundamental part of high school geometry, helping students understand the relationships within triangles and laying the groundwork for more advanced topics in mathematics. Angle bisectors are also used in various fields, such as engineering, computer graphics, and robotics, where precise calculations of angles and distances are crucial.

1.5 Relationship between Geometric Objects

First, let's investigate the relationship between a point and a line.

(1) First, a point A is on a line l. (Equivalently, a line l passes through A.)

(2) On the other hand, a point B is not on a line l. (A line l does not pass through B.)

REMARK

If the point is NOT on the line, always draw

either PARALLEL line or PERPENDICULAR line!

How about the relationship between two lines on a plane?

(1) They meet at a point or infinitely many points.

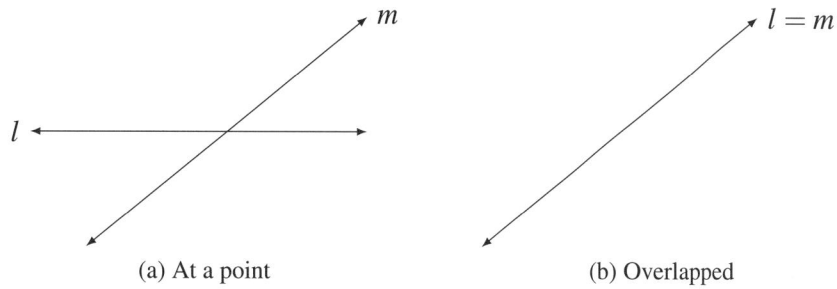

(a) At a point   (b) Overlapped

(2) Or, They do not meet.

Using the knowledge we obtained from previous page, we may conclude there are four possible cases to count when we look at how to form a plane.

1. Three non-collinear points form a unique plane.

2. A line and a point off the line form a unique plane.

3. Two non-parallel lines form a unique plane.

4. Two parallel lines form a unique plane.

How about a relationship between two lines in space?

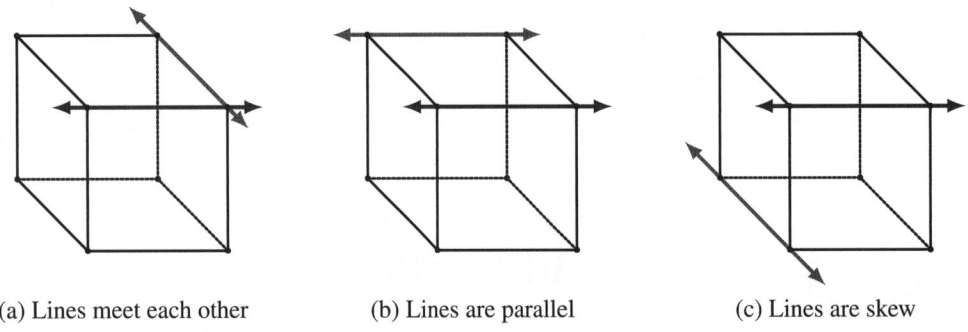

(a) Lines meet each other (b) Lines are parallel (c) Lines are skew

How about a plane and a line in a space? They either meet or don't. Look at the following figures.

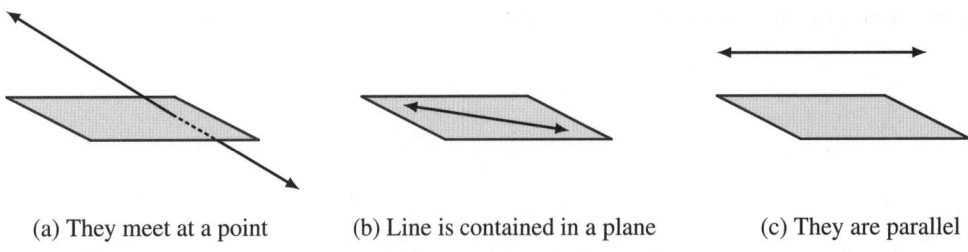

(a) They meet at a point (b) Line is contained in a plane (c) They are parallel

As one can easily check from the figure above, the number of intersection between a line and a plane in a space could be either finite or infinite. Here is a new vocabulary to learn. When a line and a plane have one point of intersection, there is an angle formed by the line and the plane, which is known as *dihedral* angle.

Lastly, two planes in a space either meet or don't. Look at the following figures.

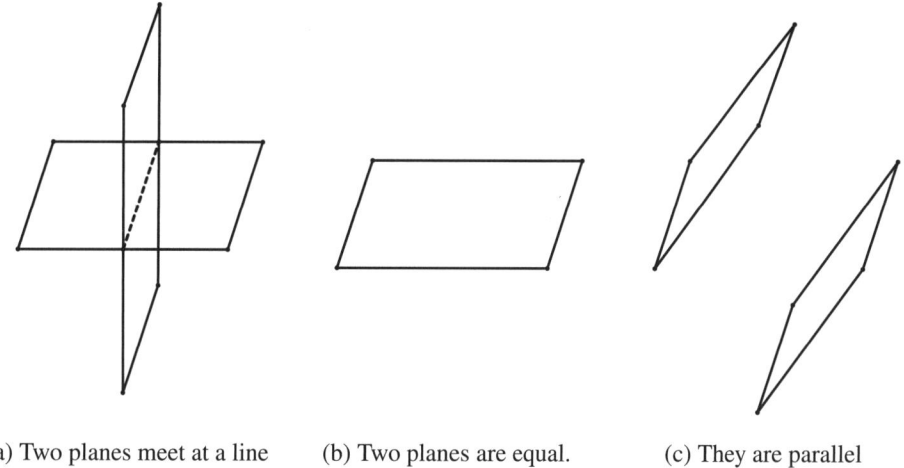

(a) Two planes meet at a line   (b) Two planes are equal.   (c) They are parallel

Example 15

Determine whether the following statement is true.

If two lines are not parallel, they should intersect at a point.

Example 16

What is the distance between $(0,0)$ and the line $y = 3$?

Example 17

What is the distance between $(3,4)$ and the line $y = 2x+1$? (Other than the solution illustrated below, graph the line to figure out the exact distance, using the notion learned in Algebra 1.)

Here is the short solution to the three examples above.

Example 15. False. If two lines are on a plane, this is true. But, if two lines are not on a plane, this may not be true. Think about skew lines. Since there is no condition on where these lines lie, it must be false.

Example 16. The distance between $(0,0)$ and the line $y = 3$ is 3 because the perpendicular distance from $(0,0)$ to the line $y = 3$ is indeed 3.

Example 17. Here is the formula to find the distance between a point and a line. First, rewrite $y = 2x+1$ into $2x-y+1 = 0$. Second, apply the formula

$$\frac{|2(3)-(4)+1|}{\sqrt{2^2+(-1)^2}} = \frac{3}{\sqrt{5}} = \frac{3\sqrt{5}}{5}$$

HISTORICAL FACT

The formula for the distance between a point and a line has its roots in classical geometry, with its earliest concepts introduced by Greek mathematicians such as Euclid and Apollonius. While Euclid's "Element" laid the groundwork for understanding perpendicularity and distances, Apolloniuss work on conic sections involved the study of distances from points to curves and lines, which indirectly contributed to this formula.

In the 17th century, René Descartes revolutionized geometry by introducing the Cartesian coordinate system. Using this framework, the modern formula for the distance from a point to a line in 2D space was derived, combining algebraic methods with geometric principles. This allowed for precise computation of distances, integral to the development of analytic geometry.

Postulates about Points, Lines, and Planes

Postulates, or axioms, are statements that describe the fundamental relationship between the basic elements of Geometry. Postulates are accepted as true without proving. School teachers may refer to them with different names or titles, but their nature does not change. Other than vertical angle postulate covered in the previous section, here are more lists of postulates related to points, lines and planes.

Postulate about the Unique Existence of Line

There is only one line through any two distinct points.

Postulate about Two Points on Line

There are at least two points on a line.

Postulate about Point of Intersection

Two distinct lines intersect at a point, if any.

Postulate about the Unique Existence of Plane

There is only one plane through any three non-collinear points.

Postulate about Three Points in Plane

There are at least three points in a plane.

Postulate about Line in Plane

Given two distinct points in a plane, there is a line on the plane, containing the two points.

Postulate about Line of Intersection

Two distinct planes intersect at a line, if any.

HISTORICAL FACT

Postulates are fundamental assumptions in mathematics, first formalized by Euclid in his "Elements" around 300 BCE. They are statements accepted without proof and serve as the foundation for logical reasoning in geometry. Euclids five postulates became the basis for what is now known as Euclidean geometry, influencing mathematical thought for centuries.

In the 19th century, the study of postulates was expanded with the development of non-Euclidean geometry by mathematicians like Lobachevsky and Riemann. They challenged Euclids fifth postulate, which led to new geometrical systems where the sum of angles in a triangle can differ from 180 degrees. This revolutionized the field of geometry and paved the way for modern mathematical theories.

Walk-Through Practices

1. How many different lines can be formed from the four points on the given circle?

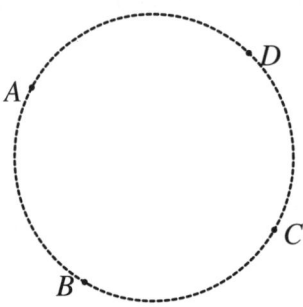

2. Convert the following geometric figures into mathematical symbols.

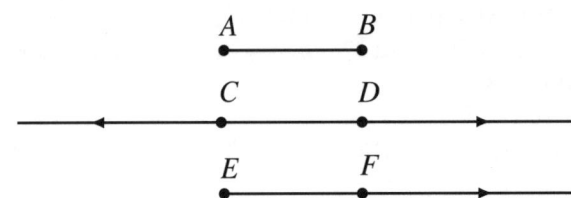

3. What is the measure of $\overline{XY}$ if X is the midpoint of $\overline{WY}$, where $WX = 3x - 3$ and $XY = 12 - 2x$?

4. Find the distance between points at $(4, 11)$ and $(-2, 3)$.

5. Suppose $\overline{XY}$ has endpoints $X(3, 8)$ and $Y(-5, -12)$. If a point W lies between X and Y such that $XW = \dfrac{1}{3}XY$, find the coordinate of W.

6. Find the measure of x, if $m\angle AOC = 90°$.

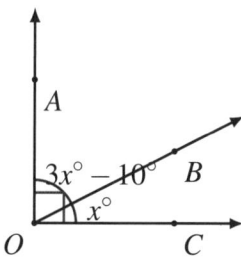

7. Determine the following angle pair relationships.

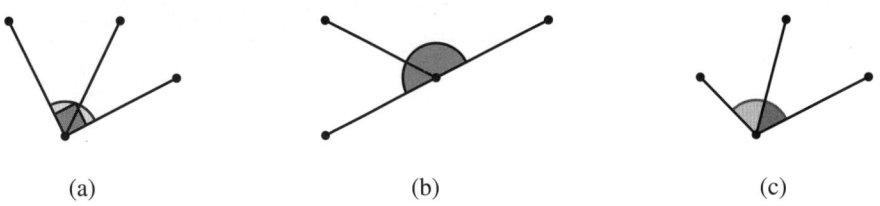

(a)   (b)   (c)

8. Look at the figure. Answer the following questions.

(a) Which of the points are on the line l?

(b) Which of the points are NOT on the line l?

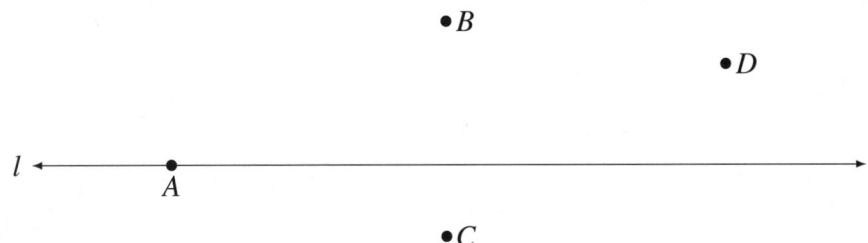

9. If $m\angle A = m\angle B = 90°$, then which of the following lines containing edges, or edges of the figure is

(a) parallel to a line $\overleftrightarrow{AD}$? Find a line containing the edges of the quadrilateral.

(b) intersecting with a line $\overleftrightarrow{AB}$?

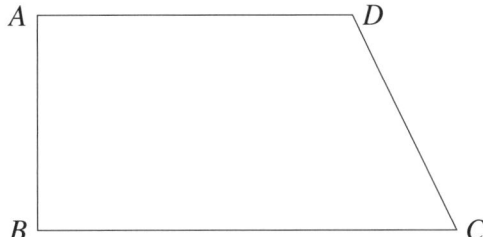

10. There are four non-collinear points A, B, C, and D, known as vertices of the solid. Such figure is known as tetrahedron. How many different planes are formed by selecting three vertices out of four?

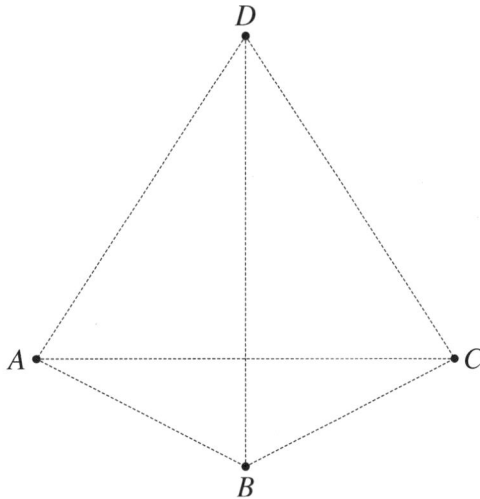

11. Look at the figure below to answer the following questions.

(a) Find lines, containing the edges of the cube, parallel to line $\overleftrightarrow{AB}$.

(b) Find lines, containing the edges of the cube, skew to line $\overleftrightarrow{BC}$.

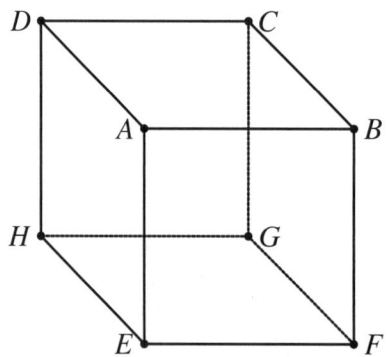

12. Find the edge(s) of the right solid, perpendicular to the plane *ABC* in the following figure.

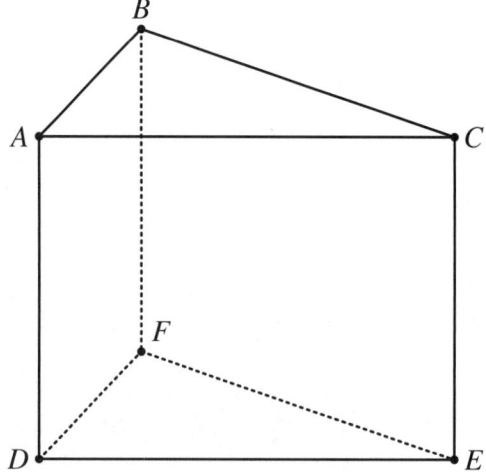

13. Find pairs of faces of the solid that are parallel to one another, where the solid is *right*.

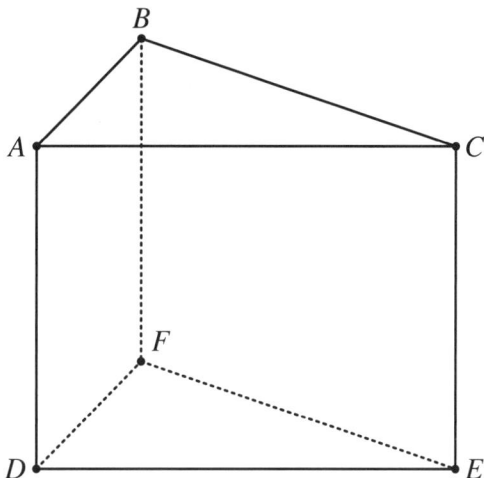

Solutions to walk-through practices can be found in the solution manual. Go to page 225.

Skill Practice

Problem 1
In how many ways can $\overline{AB}$ be represented as the same segment, including the given expression?

Problem 2
If points A, B, and C are collinear, how many distinct lines will pass the three points altogether?

Problem 3
How many edges does a cube have?

Problem 4
In how many ways can one connect two different vertices of a regular undecagon?

Problem 5
Given a regular pentagon, connect two different vertices altogether. How many different regions are formed inside the pentagon?

Problem 6
What is the measure of a straight angle, in degrees?

Problem 7
Find the exact coordinates of midpoint between $(10, 14)$ and $(16, 22)$.

Problem 8
Given two distinct points A and B, there exists a midpoint X of $\overline{AB}$, where $BX = 5$. What is the value of AB?

Problem 9
Given three different points A, B and C, if $AB = 4$, $BC = 5$, and A, B, and C are collinear, in the written order, evaluate the exact value of AC.

Problem 10
Given three distinct points A, B and C, if $AB = -4 - 3x$ and $BC = 2 - 6x$, then $AB = BC$ cannot happen because the lengths AB and BC are unusual. What is this unusual value?

Answer Key

1. 2

2. 1

3. 12

4. 55

5. 11

6. 180°

7. (13, 18)

8. 10

9. 9

10. −10

38   The Essential Guide to Geometry

Topic 2
Mathematical Reasoning

2.1 Induction and Deduction 40
2.2 Algebraic Proof and Geometric Proof 45
2.3 Basic Postulates for Segments and Angles 46

2.1 Induction and Deduction

(1) Inductive reasoning is a conjecture based on observations and patterns. There could be *counterexample* that shows that the conjecture is false.

(2) Deductive reasoning uses postulates, definitions, properties, or theorems to reach logical conclusion.

(3) A statement, represented by p, is a sentence that is either true or false. Truth value tells us whether p is true or false.

(4) The negation of the statement p is the opposite of p, along with opposite truth value of p. We write $\neg p$.

(5) *Conjunction* is a compound statement by joining two or more statements with *and*. On the other hand, *disjunction* is a compound statement by joining two or more statements with *or*.

Here is the truth table for conjunction, and disjunction.

p	q	$p \cap q$
T	T	T
T	F	F
F	T	F
F	F	F

(a) Conjunction

p	q	$p \cup q$
T	T	T
T	F	T
F	T	T
F	F	F

(b) Disjunction

Let's learn what a conditional statement looks like. It has hypothesis and conclusion.

$$\text{If } p, \text{ then } q.$$

where p is hypothesis and q is conclusion. We can paraphrase this *if-then* form into

- $p \implies q$.
- p implies q.

There are related conditionals : converse, inverse and contrapositive.

1. Conditional : If p, then q.
2. Converse of the conditional : If q, then p.
3. Inverse of the conditional : If $\neg p$, then $\neg q$.
4. Contrapositive of the conditional : If $\neg q$, then $\neg p$.

The truth value for the original statement and its contrapositive are equal.

Example 18

A conditional statement has _____ of *TRUE* or *FALSE*. Fill the blank.

Example 19

Use inductive reasoning to figure out the value of x for the list of integers $\{1, 3, 5, 7, x\}$.

Example 20

Write a contrapositive statement for the following conditional statement : If x is real, then $x^2 \geq 0$.

Here is the short solution to the three examples above.

Example 18. A conditional statement has *truth value* of *TRUE* or *FALSE*.

Example 19. The value of x is 9. Consecutive difference is 2, so we expect to have the value of x as 9.

Example 20. Its contrapositive goes like this. If $x^2 < 0$, then x is not real.

Now, we say that statements with the same truth values are *logically equivalent*. This is important when we prove mathematical statements using deduction. Here is the table that summarizes what happens.

p	q	$p \implies q$	$q \implies p$	$\neg p \implies \neg q$	$\neg q \implies \neg p$
T	T	T	T	T	T
T	F	F	T	T	F
F	T	T	F	F	T
F	F	T	T	T	T

A *biconditional statement* is the conjunction of a conditional statement and its converse. We write $p \iff q$, and we read p if and only if q. Sometimes, if and only if is abbreviated as iff.

For instance, $x = 2$ iff $x^2 = 4$. Let's analyze the conditional statement and its converse.

1. Conditional : If $x = 2$, then $x^2 = 4$. This is true.

2. Converse : If $x^2 = 4$, then $x = 2$. This is false.

Therefore, the biconditional statement is false. Now, last but not least, we need to talk about the tools for deduction. In particular, there are two tools for deductive reasoning.

1. Law of Detachment : If $p \implies q$ is true and p is true, then q is true.

2. Law of Syllogism : If $p \implies q$ is true and $q \implies r$ is true, then $p \implies r$ is also true.

HISTORICAL FACT

The Law of Syllogism, originating from Aristotelian logic, states that if "A implies B" and "B implies C," then "A implies C." This logical principle is foundational in deductive reasoning and is widely applied in mathematics, philosophy, and computer science for constructing valid arguments and proofs.

The law of detachment and the law of syllogism are widely used in logic, which means they are important tools of logical deduction in reading comprehension as well.

Example 21

If $x^2 = 1$, then $x = 1$. Find whether the conditional statement are true or false.

Example 22

Prove that $x = 3$ iff $2x - 3 = 3$.

Example 23

Find any counterexample to the following false statement : If x and y are even integers, then $x + y$ is odd.

Example 24

Assume that it is true that if it's Tuesday, then it must be rainy. Today is Tuesday. What can you tell about the weather? Illustrate your reasoning either by the law of detachment or law of syllogism.

Here is the solution to examples covered in the previous page.

Example 21. We only have to figure when $x^2 = 1$ but $x \neq 1$. Assume $x^2 = 1$ is true. Then, $x = \pm 1$. If $x = -1$, then the hypothesis is still true, but $-1 \neq 1$. Therefore, the conditional statement is false.

Example 22. Assume that $x = 3$. Then, $2(3) - 3 = 6 - 3 = 3$, so $(\Rightarrow)$ is true. On the other hand, assume that $2x - 3 = 3$. Then, $2x = 6$, so $x = 3$. Therefore, $(\Leftarrow)$ is also true. Therefore, $x = 3$ if and only if $2x - 3 = 3$.

Example 23. Any pair of even integers would suffice. For instance, let $x = 2$ and $y = 4$. Then, $x + y = 6$, which is not odd. At least one counterexample proves that the original statement is false.

Example 24. Look at the first sentence. The conditional statement is true. Since the hypothesis is satisfied, the conclusion must be satisfied. Therefore, you can tell that it is rainy, according to the law of detachment.

HISTORICAL FACT

The foundations of formal logic, including the Law of Detachment and the Law of Syllogism, can be traced back to ancient Greece around 300 BCE. Aristotle, in his works on syllogistic logic, laid the groundwork for these principles. The Law of Detachment, also known as modus ponens, and the Law of Syllogism were crucial in developing deductive reasoning, influencing both philosophy and mathematics. These laws continue to play a central role in modern logical systems and computational theories.

In modern computer science, both laws are fundamental to programming and algorithm design. The Law of Detachment is applied in conditional statements (e.g., if-then structures), allowing programs to execute specific actions based on true conditions. The Law of Syllogism is used in chaining logical deductions, crucial for decision-making algorithms, artificial intelligence, and database query systems. These logical principles enable computers to process complex chains of reasoning efficiently.

Moreover, these logical laws are also foundational in constructing proofs in formal verification processes, where algorithms are rigorously tested for correctness. By ensuring that each step follows logical principles, software engineers can verify that programs behave as expected in all possible scenarios, reducing the likelihood of bugs or system failures. This application is critical in fields like cybersecurity, embedded systems, and complex systems automation.

The biconditional statement, expressed as "if and only if" (IFF), is another key logical structure used in both mathematics and computer science. It indicates that two statements are both necessary and sufficient for one another. In programming, biconditional logic helps verify whether two conditions are logically equivalent, ensuring that one condition holds true if and only if the other does, often used in algorithms that require symmetry or equivalence checks.

2.2 Algebraic Proof and Geometric Proof

Algebraic proof uses the property of equality to solve an equation with a step-by-step approach to the given conditional statement. The following rules are real number properties.

1. Reflexive : For every $x \in \mathbb{R}$, it is true that $x = x$.

2. Symmetric : For every $x, y \in \mathbb{R}$, if $x = y$, then $y = x$.

3. Transitive : For every $x, y, z \in \mathbb{R}$, if $x = y$ and $y = z$, then $x = z$.

4. Translation(+) : For every $x, y, z \in \mathbb{R}$, if $x = y$, then $x \pm z = y \pm z$.

5. Translation($\times$) : For every $x, y, z \in \mathbb{R}$, if $x = y$, then $xz = yz$. If $z \neq 0$, then $\dfrac{x}{z} = \dfrac{y}{z}$.

6. Substitution : For every $x, y \in \mathbb{R}$, if $x = y$, then x can be replaced by y for any equation or expression.

7. Distributive : For every $x, y, z \in \mathbb{R}$, then $x(y + z) = xy + xz$.

Geometric proof uses the first three properties most. Look at the following tables.

Property	Segments
Reflexive	$XY = XY$
Symmetric	If $XY = UV$, then $UV = XY$.
Transitive	If $XY = UV$ and $UV = WZ$, then $XY = WZ$.

(a) Segments

Property	Angles
Reflexive	$m\angle X = m\angle X$
Symmetric	If $m\angle X = m\angle Y$, then $m\angle Y = m\angle X$.
Transitive	If $m\angle X = m\angle Y$ and $m\angle Y = m\angle Z$, then $m\angle X = m\angle Z$.

(b) Angles

What one should know in school Geometry, two-column proofs usually start with geometric objects, bring their arguments to algebraic properties, and conclude with geometric properties. For instance, if someone should show that $\overline{AB} \cong \overline{CD}$, then one should use the definition of congruent segments to show that $AB = CD$, and then return to $\overline{AB} \cong \overline{CD}$. When we prove theorems, we change segments or angles into their measures to use the property of equality(algebraic properties) and we come back to the angle congruence or properties using postulates or definitions.

2.3 Basic Postulates for Segments and Angles

First, there are two postulates we use for proving properties about segments.

Ruler Postulate

1. Point on a line has $1-1$ correspondence to a real number, which is the coordinate of point.

2. Distance between two points, i.e., A and B, is the absolute value of the difference of coordinates, represented by the line segment between A and B.

Segment Addition Postulate

1. Given points X, Z and Y between X and Z, then $XZ = XY + YZ$.

2. If $XZ = XY + YZ$, then Y is between X and Z.

Likewise, the following two postulates are basic postulates for proving angle relationships.

Protractor Postulate

1. Each angle has $1-1$ correspondence to real numbers from 0 to 180.

2. The angle measure is equal to the absolute value of the difference between the real numbers for rays.

Angle Addition Postulate

If Y is an interior point of $\angle WXZ$, then $m\angle WXZ = m\angle WXY + m\angle YXZ$.

Conventionally, ruler postulate and protractor postulate show that there is exactly one-to-one correspondence between geometric object and real number. This is the reason why two-column proofs would work, in fact. Otherwise, how on earth would you connect algebraic proof with geometric proof? That being written, here is what one must know to proceed on the journey of two-column proofs.

- Definition of Congruent Angles : Angles are congruent if and only if their measures are equal.

- Definition of Congruent Segments : Segments are congruent if and only if their measures are equal.

- Vertical Angle Postulate : If angles are vertical, then they are congruent.

- Definition of Right Angle : Angle is right if and only if its measure is 90°. (One can similarly set up definition of acute angle or obtuse angle.)

- Definition of Complementary Angles : Angle A and B are complementary if and only if their sum of measures equals 90°.

- Definition of Supplementary Angles : Angle A and B are supplementary if and only if their sum of measures equals 180°.

- Definition of Linear Pair : Angle A and B are linear pair if and only if they are adjacent and supplementary.

Example 25

Given two points X, Z, if Y is NOT between X and Z, then what happens to $XZ = XY + YZ$?

Example 26

If $\overrightarrow{AO}$ bisects $\angle BAC$, $m\angle BAO = 4x + 28$ and $m\angle AOC = 5x + 14$, then find $m\angle BAC$.

Here is the solution to the examples above.

Example 25. $XZ < XY + YZ$ by triangular inequality, the definition of which will be covered in detail in a different chapter.

Example 26. By Angle Addition Postulate, $m\angle BAC = m\angle BAO + m\angle AOC = 9x + 42$. Since, $\overrightarrow{AO}$ bisects $\angle BAC$, we get $4x + 28 = 5x + 14$, so $x = 14$. Therefore, $m\angle BAC = 9(14) + 42 = 168°$.

Walk-Through Practices

14. Use the following statements to write a compound statement for conjunction and disjunction.

- $p: 5+(-5)=0$
- $q:$ Natural numbers are all even.

15. Complete the truth table below.

p	q	$\neg p$	$\neg p \cup q$
T	T		
T	F		
F	T		
F	F		

16. Determine the truth value of the following conditional statement for each set of conditions : If *John receives perfect score on his Geometry final,* then *he will receive A for Geometry.*

(a) John really got perfect score ; he received A for Geometry.

(b) John got perfect score ; he did not receive A for Geometry.

(c) John did not get perfect score ; he received A for Geometry.

(d) John did not get perfect score ; he did not receive A for Geometry.

17. Two lines are parallel if and only if they do not meet. Determine whether this biconditional statement is true.

18. Determine whether the statement (3) follows from the statements (1) and (2) by the law of detachment or the law of syllogism.

(a)
(1) straight angles are congruent.

(2) $\angle X \cong \angle Y$

(3) $\angle X$ and $\angle Y$ are straight angles.

(b)
(1) straight angles are congruent.

(2) $\angle X$ and $\angle Y$ are straight angles.

(3) $\angle X$ and $\angle Y$ are congruent.

19. Prove that segment congruence is reflexive, symmetric, and transitive. Fill the blanks.

(1) Reflexive : $\overline{AB} \cong \overline{AB}$.

Statement	Reason
1. $\overline{AB} \cong \overline{AB}$.	1.
2.	2. Definition of Congruent Segments
3. $\overline{AB} \cong \overline{AB}$.	3.

(2) Symmetric : if $\overline{AB} \cong \overline{CD}$, then $\overline{CD} \cong \overline{AB}$.

Statement	Reason
1. $\overline{AB} \cong \overline{CD}$.	1.
2. $AB = CD$.	2.
3. $CD = AB$.	3.
4. $\overline{CD} \cong \overline{AB}$.	4.

(3) Transitive : if $\overline{AB} \cong \overline{CD}$ and $\overline{CD} \cong \overline{EF}$, then $\overline{AB} \cong \overline{EF}$.

Statement	Reason
1. $\overline{AB} \cong \overline{CD}, \overline{CD} \cong \overline{EF}$.	1.
2. $AB = CD, CD = EF$.	2.
3.	3.
4. $\overline{AB} \cong \overline{EF}$.	4.

20. Prove that if $3(x-2) = 6$, then $x = 4$ by two-column proof. In particular, fill the reasoning part.

Statement	Reason
1. $3(x-2) = 6$.	1.
2. $3x - 6 = 6$.	2.
3. $3x = 12$.	3.
4. $x = 4$.	4.

21. If A, B, C are collinear in this order, prove that $AB = AC - BC$.

Statement	Reason
1. A, B, and C are collinear, in the written order.	1. Given
2. $AC = AB + BC$.	2. Segment Addition Postulate
3.	3. Translation Property by Subtraction
4. $AB = AC - BC$.	4.

22. If $\overline{AB} \cong \overline{AC}$ and $AB = 4$, prove that $AC = 4$.

Statement	Reason
1. $\overline{AB} \cong \overline{AC}$, $AB = 4$.	1.
2. $AB = AC$, $AB = 4$.	2.
3. $AC = 4$.	3.

23. Prove that if two angles form a linear pair, then they are supplementary angles. In other words, if $\angle A$ and $\angle B$ form a linear pair, then they are supplementary.

Statement	Reason
1. $\angle A$ and $\angle B$ form a linear pair.	1.
2. $m\angle A + m\angle B = 180°$.	2.
3. $\angle A$ and $\angle B$ are supplementary.	3.

24. Prove that if the non-common sides of two adjacent angles form a right angle, then they are complementary angles. For notational convenience, assume that these two adjacent angles are called $\angle X$ and $\angle Y$. Also, call such the right angle as $\angle C$.

Statement	Reason
1. $\angle X$ and $\angle Y$ form $\angle C$.	1.
2. $m\angle X + m\angle Y = m\angle C$.	2.
3. $m\angle C = 90°$.	3.
4. $m\angle X + m\angle Y = 90°$.	4.
5. $\angle X$ and $\angle Y$ are complementary.	5.

25. Angles supplementary to the same angle (or to congruent angles) are congruent. In other words, if $m\angle A + m\angle B = 180°$ and $m\angle C + m\angle B = 180°$, then $\angle A \cong \angle C$.

Statement	Reason
1. $m\angle A + m\angle B = 180°$, $m\angle C + m\angle B = 180°$	1.
2. $m\angle A + m\angle B = m\angle C + m\angle B$.	2.
3. $m\angle A = m\angle C$.	3.
4. $\angle A \cong \angle C$.	4.

26. Angles complementary to the same angle (or to congruent angles) are congruent. In other words, if $m\angle A + m\angle B = 90°$ and $m\angle C + m\angle B = 90°$, then $\angle A \cong \angle C$. (This is a twin practice of the previous problem. Replicate the same process in the two-column proof.)

Statement	Reason
1.	1.
2.	2.
3.	3.
4.	4.

27. If two angles are vertical angles, then they are congruent. In particular, show that ∠1 is congruent to ∠3. (In this example, we actually show that vertical angle postulate can also be proved!)

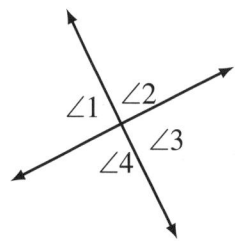

Statement	Reason
1. ∠1 and ∠2 form a linear pair. ∠2 and ∠3 form a linear pair.	1. Given
2.	2. Definition of Linear Pair
3. $m\angle 1 + m\angle 2 = m\angle 2 + m\angle 3$.	3.
4. $m\angle 1 = m\angle 3$.	4.
5. ∠1 ≅ ∠3.	5.

28. Show that perpendicular lines intersect to form right angles. In other words, if lines l and m are perpendicular, then the angle formed by l and m, call it ∠X, is right. Call other angles Y, Z and W. Assume that Y and X form adjacent angles, Z is vertical angle of Y, and W a vertical angle of X, respectively.

Statement	Reason
1. l and m are perpendicular. Y and X form a linear pair.	1. Given
2. ∠X is right.	2.
3. $m\angle X = 90°$.	3.
4. $m\angle Y + m\angle X = 180°$.	4. Definition of Linear Pair
5. $m\angle Y + 90° = 180°$.	5.
6. $m\angle Y = 90°$.	6. Translation Property by Subtraction
7. $m\angle Y = m\angle Z$ and $m\angle X = m\angle W$.	7.
8. $m\angle Z = 90°$ and $m\angle W = 90°$.	8.
9. ∠X, ∠Y, ∠Z, and ∠W are right angles.	9.

29. Prove that all right angles are congruent. In other words, if ∠A and ∠B are both right angles, then they are congruent.

Statement	Reason
1. ∠A and ∠B are right angles.	1. Given
2. $m\angle A = 90°$ and $m\angle B = 90°$.	2.
3. $m\angle A = m\angle B$.	3.
4. $\angle A \cong \angle B$.	4.

30. Show that perpendicular lines form congruent adjacent angles. In other words, let l and m be the perpendicular lines, and ∠X and ∠Y be the adjacent angles, a linear pair formed by the intersection. Prove that ∠X and ∠Y are congruent.

Statement	Reason
1. l and m are perpendicular. ∠X and ∠Y form a linear pair.	1. Given
2. ∠X is right.	2.
3. $m\angle X = 90°$.	3.
4. $m\angle X + m\angle Y = 180°$.	4.
5. $90° + m\angle Y = 180°$.	5.
6. $m\angle Y = 90°$.	6.
7. $m\angle X = m\angle Y$.	7.
8. $\angle X \cong \angle Y$.	8.

31. Prove that if two angles ∠X and ∠Y are congruent and supplementary, then each angle is a right angle.

Statement	Reason
1. ∠X and ∠Y are congruent, and supplementary.	1. Given
2. $m\angle X = m\angle Y$.	2.
3. $m\angle X + m\angle Y = 180°$.	3.
4. $m\angle X + m\angle X = 180°$.	4.
5. $m\angle X = 90°$.	5. Translation Property of Division
6. $m\angle Y = 90°$.	6.
7. ∠X and ∠Y are right angles.	7.

Topic_1 Basic Elements of Geometry

32. Show that if two congruent angles $\angle X$ and $\angle Y$ form a linear pair, then they are right angles. (Replicate the same procedure as the previous problem.)

Statement	Reason
1. $\angle X$ and $\angle Y$ are congruent, and they form a linear pair.	1. Given
2.	2.
3.	3.
4.	4.
5.	5.
6.	6.
7.	7.

Solutions to walk-through practices can be found in the solution manual. Go to page 225.

Skill Practice

Problem 1
Using inductive reasoning, deduce the value of x for the following sequence :
$\{1,3,5,7,9,11,x,\cdots\}$.

Problem 2
Write the converse of the following mathematical statement : If $x = 1$, then $x^2 = 1$.

Problem 3
If $x = 1$, then $x+2 = 3$. If $x+2 = 3$, then $x+4 = 5$. According to the law of syllogism, write down a mathematical statement.

Problem 4
Write down the property used in the following statements : If $a = b$, then $b = a$.

Problem 5
Write down the property used in the following statements : If $a = b$ and $b = c$, then $a = c$.

Problem 6
If A, B, and C are collinear, in the written order, where $AB = 3$ and $BC = 4$, find AC.

Problem 7
Which postulate is used to solve the previous problem 6?

Problem 8
If angles are vertical, they are congruent. Name the postulate when we address this property.

Problem 9
Assume $x = 3$. If $y + x = 5$, then $y + 3 = 5$. Which property is used in this procedure?

Problem 10
If $\overline{AB} \cong \overline{CD}$, then $AB = CD$. Which definition is used in this statement?

Answer Key

1. 13

2. If $x^2 = 1$, then $x = 1$.

3. If $x = 1$, then $x + 4 = 5$.

4. Symmetric property

5. Transitive property

6. 7

7. Segment Addition Postulate

8. Vertical Angle Postulate

9. Substitution property

10. Definition of Congruent Segments

BEFORE YOU MOVE ON

Transitive Property vs. Substitution Property

Transitive Property: The transitive property states that if two quantities are equal to a third quantity, then they are equal to each other. Formally, if:

$$a = b \quad \text{and} \quad b = c, \quad \text{then} \quad a = c.$$

Example: If $x = 5$ and $5 = y$, then $x = y$. This property emphasizes the logical progression of equality.

Substitution Property: The substitution property allows one to replace a quantity with another quantity to which it is equal. Formally, if:

$$a = b, \quad \text{then } a \text{ can be replaced by } b \text{ in any equation or expression.}$$

Example: If $x = 3$ and $y = x + 2$, substituting x with 3 gives $y = 3 + 2 = 5$. This property focuses on replacing variables or terms to simplify expressions or solve equations.

Key Difference:

- **Transitive Property** establishes a direct relationship of equality between three quantities.

- **Substitution Property** focuses on replacing one equal quantity with another within a specific context.

Analogy: Think of the transitive property as a "bridge" connecting three elements, while substitution is like "swapping" one element for another to simplify or progress in solving a problem.

Topic 3

Parallel and Perpendicular Lines

3.1 Parallel Lines and Transversal..60
3.2 Distance Formula Revisited...63

3.1 Parallel Lines and Transversal

We learned what parallel lines and planes look like in the first topic. Now, let's look at the following figures to understand transversals and angles.

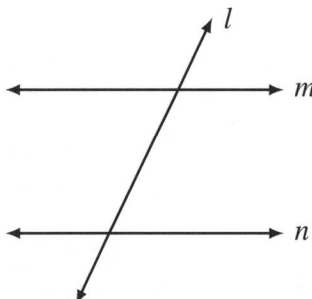

where a line l is a transversal to the two parallel lines m and n. Now, one may learn about the important postulates describing line relationships by comparing specific angles.

Talking about lines, one may compute their slopes using Algebra 1 knowledge. The slope s of a line containing two points (x_1, y_1) and (x_2, y_2) is given by

$$s = \frac{y_2 - y_1}{x_2 - x_1}$$

where $x_2 \neq x_1$. The line equation has the form of $y = mx + b$ where m is the slope and b is the y-intercept. Here is the point-slope form, which generalizes the intercept form

$$y = m(x - a) + b$$

where the line passes through (a, b). Of course, one may come up with some extra postulates about slopes.

Parallel Line Slope Postulate
Two non-vertical parallel lines have the same slope.

Perpendicular Line Slope Postulate
Two non-vertical perpendicular lines have the product of their slopes -1.

In the next page, we cover more examples related to Algebra 1 materials related to these two postulates.

Example 27

Find the line equation whose *y*-intercept is 3 and slope is 4.

Example 28

Find the slope of a line passing through two points $(2,3)$ and $(5,3)$.

Example 29

If the line *l* has the slope of 3, determine the slope of its perpendicular line.

Example 30

If $y = mx + b$ is parallel to a line $y = 5x - 3$, find the exact value of *m*.

Example 31

Suppose there is a horizontal line $y = 3$. Find the line equation that is perpendicular to $y = 3$, passing through $(2,3)$.

Here is the solution to the problems in the previous page.

Example 27. Using the point-slope form, we get $y = 4(x-0)+3 = 4x+3$. Sometimes, it is convenient for us to just write $y = mx+b$ where b is the y-intercept and m is the slope value.

Example 28. The slope of a line passing through $(2,3)$ and $(5,3)$ is $\dfrac{3-3}{5-2} = 0$.

Example 29. The slope of the perpendicular line is a negative reciprocal of 3, i.e., $-\dfrac{1}{3}$.

Example 30. Since the lines are parallel, we conclude that the value of m equals 5.

Example 31. The previous case deals with no horizontal nor perpendicular lines. What if the given line is horizontal or vertical? Horizontal line has the slope value of 0, whereas vertical line has slope undefined. A vertical line is perpendicular to the horizontal line. Since $y = 3$ is horizontal, a vertical line passing through $(2,3)$ is the perpendicular line. Therefore, $x = 2$.

Now, let's delve into the corresponding angle postulate and its converse.

> **Corresponding Angle Postulate**
> *When two parallel lines are cut by a transversal, then each pair of corresponding angles is congruent.*

> **Converse of Corresponding Angle Postulate**
> *If two lines in a plane cut by a transversal have congruent corresponding angles, then the lines are parallel.*

Before, moving onto a bit more algebraic application of parallel lines and perpendicular lines, read the following procedures which show the construction of parallel lines.

1. Use a straightedge to draw a line and label two points on the line as X and Y. Draw a point Z not on $\overleftrightarrow{XY}$ and draw $\overrightarrow{ZX}$.

2. Copy $\angle ZXY$ so that Z is the vertex of the angle. Label the intersection points M and N, where M is on $\overleftrightarrow{ZX}$.

3. Draw $\overleftrightarrow{ZN}$. They are congruent corresponding angles, so we have parallel lines.

The process shows that there is at least one parallel line passing through a point off the given line. In fact, there is only one line, which was discovered and proved by Playfair. Here we provide it as a postulate.

> **Unique Parallel Line Postulate**
> *Given a line and a point off the line, there is only one line passing through the point, which is parallel to the given line.*

3.2 Distance Formula Revisited

In school Geometry course, we normally use two forms of distance formula.

- Quadratic Form : the usual distance formula addressed by Pythagorean Theorem.

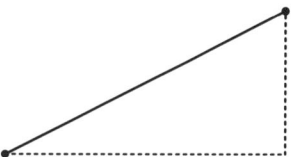

- Linear Form : only for vertical line and horizontal line, where one may simply find the difference between the coordinates. This happens when the *x*-coordinates are unchanged, or *y*-coordinates are unchanged.

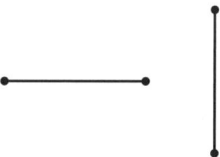

The distance between a point and a line is the length of the segment perpendicular to the line from the point. On the other hand, the distance between two parallel lines is the length of the perpendicular segment with endpoints lying on each of the two lines.

Example 32

Find the distance between $(4,3)$ and $(-3,3)$.

Example 33

Find the distance between $(-7,-3)$ and the *y*-axis.

Here is the solution to examples covered in the previous page.

Example 32. Instead of using the distance formula, since y-coordinates are fixed, we simply look at the difference of x-coordinates, which is equal to 7.

Example 33. By plotting $(-7, -3)$ on a coordinate plane, we find out that 7 is the horizontal distance between $(-7, -3)$ and the y-axis. Hence, the distance is 7 unit. On the other hand, the distance between $(-7, -3)$ and the x-axis is 3.

HISTORICAL FACT

The concept of distance has evolved into various mathematical metrics to suit different contexts and applications. While the Euclidean distance, derived from the Pythagorean theorem, is the most familiar, other distance formulas offer alternative perspectives.

One notable example is the taxicab metric, also called Manhattan distance, where the distance between two points is the sum of the absolute differences of their coordinates. Unlike Euclidean distance, it measures paths constrained to grid-like movements, making it ideal for urban planning and computer algorithms.

The Chebyshev distance, often used in chess, calculates the maximum difference between coordinates, reflecting the movement of a king on a chessboard. Similarly, the Minkowski distance generalizes both Euclidean and taxicab metrics, with an adjustable parameter allowing for diverse applications.

In higher dimensions, the Mahalanobis distance accounts for correlations between variables, widely applied in statistics and machine learning. Another intriguing metric is the Hamming distance, which measures the number of differing positions in strings or binary data, crucial in coding theory and error detection.

In topology, the Hausdorff distance measures how far two subsets of a metric space are from each other, often used in image recognition and 3D modeling. The Wasserstein distance, also known as Earth Movers Distance, quantifies the effort to transform one probability distribution into another, playing a key role in optimal transport and data analysis.

These diverse distance metrics emphasize the flexibility and innovation in mathematical thinking. Each metric adapts to unique requirements, from analyzing statistical relationships to understanding spatial structures, demonstrating how foundational concepts like distance evolve to meet the needs of science and technology.

Walk-Through Practices

33. Identify angle relationships for the following figure.

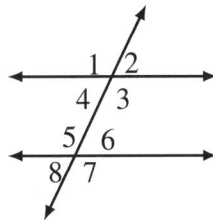

34. If two parallel lines are cut by a transversal, then each pair of alternate interior angles is congruent. In particular, in the figure below, if lines m and l are parallel, show that $\angle B$ and $\angle C$ are congruent.

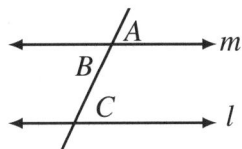

Statement	Reason
1. Line m and l are parallel.	1. Given
2. $\angle A \cong \angle C$.	2.
3. $\angle A \cong \angle B$.	3.
4. $\angle B \cong \angle C$.	4.

Topic_1 Basic Elements of Geometry

35. Prove the statement : if two parallel lines are cut by a transversal, then each pair of consecutive interior angles is supplementary. In particular, if lines m and l are parallel, then $\angle B$ and $\angle C$ are supplementary.

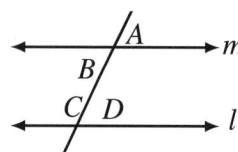

Statement	Reason
1. Line m and l are parallel. $\angle C$ and $\angle D$ form a linear pair.	1. Given
2. $\angle A \cong \angle B$.	2.
3. $\angle A \cong \angle D$.	3.
4. $\angle B \cong \angle D$.	4.
5. $m\angle C + m\angle D = 180°$.	5.
6. $m\angle C + m\angle B = 180°$.	6.
7. $\angle B$ and $\angle C$ form a linear pair.	7.

36. Prove the statement : if two parallel lines are cut by a transversal, then each pair of alternate exterior angles is congruent. In particular, if lines m and l are parallel, show that $\angle A$ and $\angle C$ are congruent.

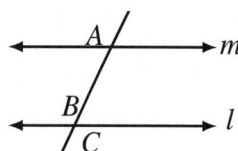

Statement	Reason
1. Line m and l are parallel.	1. Given
2. $\angle A \cong \angle B$.	2.
3. $\angle B \cong \angle C$.	3.
4. $\angle A \cong \angle C$.	4.

37. Prove that if a line is perpendicular to one of two parallel lines in a plane, then it is perpendicular to the other. In particular, if a line *m* is perpendicular to a transversal, a line *l*, which is parallel to *m*, is also perpendicular to the transversal.

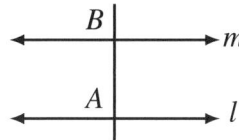

Statement	Reason
1. Line *m* and *l* are parallel. Line *m* is perpendicular to the transversal.	1. Given
2. ∠B is right.	2.
3. $m\angle B = 90°$.	3.
4. $\angle A \cong \angle B$.	4.
5. $m\angle A = m\angle B$.	5.
6. $m\angle A = 90°$.	6.
7. Line *l* is perpendicular to the transversal.	7.

38. Find the measure of *x*.

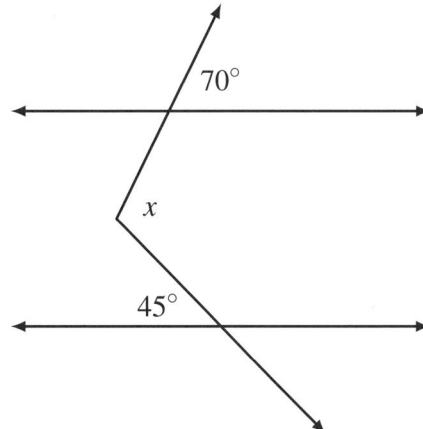

39. Find the line equation parallel to $y = 3x + 3$ that passes through $(-3, -5)$.

40. Find the slope of a line perpendicular to the line given by $4x + 8y = 12$.

41. Prove that if two lines in a plane are crossed by a transversal such that alternate exterior angles are congruent, then the two lines are parallel. In particular, if ∠A and ∠C are congruent, show that lines *l* and *m* are parallel.

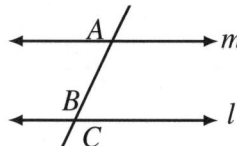

Statement	Reason
1. ∠A and ∠C are congruent.	1. Given
2. ∠A ≅ ∠C.	2.
3. ∠B ≅ ∠C.	3.
4. ∠A ≅ ∠B.	4.
5. Lines *m* and *l* are parallel.	5.

42. Prove that if two lines in a plane are crossed by a transversal such that consecutive interior angles are supplementary, then the two lines are parallel. In particular, if ∠A and ∠B are supplementary, then lines *l* and *m* are parallel.

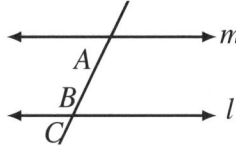

Statement	Reason
1. ∠A and ∠B are are supplementary. ∠B and ∠C form a linear pair.	1. Given
2. $m\angle A + m\angle B = 180°$.	2.
3. $m\angle B + m\angle C = 180°$.	3.
4. $m\angle A + m\angle B = m\angle B + m\angle C$.	4.
5. $m\angle A = m\angle C$.	5.
6. Lines *l* and *m* are parallel.	6.

43. Prove that if two lines in a plane are crossed by a transversal such that alternate interior angles are congruent, then the two lines are parallel. In particular, if ∠A and ∠B are congruent, then *l* and *m* are parallel.

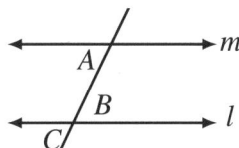

Statement	Reason
1. ∠A and ∠B are congruent.	1. Given
2. ∠A ≅ ∠B.	2.
3. ∠B ≅ ∠C.	3.
4. ∠A ≅ ∠C.	4.
5. Lines *l* and *m* are parallel.	5.

44. Prove that if two lines in a plane are perpendicular to the transversal, then they are parallel. (Refer to the figure below.)

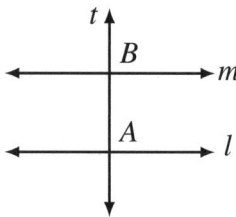

Statement	Reason
1. m and t are perpendicular. l and t are perpendicular.	1. Given
2. $\angle B$ is right. $\angle A$ is right.	2.
3. $m\angle B = 90°$. $m\angle A = 90°$.	3.
4. $m\angle A = m\angle B$.	4.
5. Lines l and m are parallel.	5.

45. Find the distance between a point and the line.

(a) $(5, 1)$ and $y = 3$ (b) $(3, 1)$ and $y = x$

46. Find the distance between $y = 2x$ and $y = 2x + 2$.

Solutions to walk-through practices can be found in the solution manual. Go to page 225.

Skill Practice

Problem 1
If angles *A* and *B* are *complementary*, where the measure of *A* equals 35°, determine the exact value of the measure of angle *B*, in degree measures.

Problem 2
If angles *C* and *D* are *supplementary*, where the measure of *C* equals 37°, determine the exact value of the measure of angle *D*, in degree measures.

Problem 3
If angles *E* and *F* form *a linear pair*, where the measure of *E* equals 50°, determine the measure of $\angle F$, in degrees.

Problem 4
Let *A* and *B* be *vertical angles*. If the measure of *A* equals 70°, determine the measure of $\angle B$, in degrees.

Problem 5
Let *X* and *Y* be *congruent angles*. If the measure of *A* equals 45°, determine the measure of $\angle Y$, in degrees.

Problem 6
Given two parallel lines and a transversal, if a measure of an angle equals 60°, what is the measure of its *alternate interior angle*, in degrees, assuming that it exists?

Problem 7
Given two parallel lines and a transversal, if a measure of an angle equals 45°, what is the measure of its *consecutive exterior angle*, in degrees, assuming that it exists?

Problem 8
Given two parallel lines and a transversal, if a measure of an angle equals 70°, what is the measure of its *alternate exterior angle*, in degrees, assuming that it exists?

Problem 9
Given two parallel lines and a transversal, if a measure of an angle equals 100°, what is the measure of its *consecutive exterior angle*, in degrees, assuming that it exists?

Problem 10
Given two parallel lines and a transversal, if a measure of an angle equals 30°, what is the measure of its *corresponding angle*, in degrees, assuming that it exists?

Answer Key

1. 65°

2. 143°

3. 130°

4. 70°

5. 45°

6. 60°

7. 135°

8. 70°

9. 80°

10. 30°

BEFORE YOU MOVE ON

Playfair's Theorem

Statement of the Theorem: Playfair's Theorem is a fundamental result in Euclidean geometry that provides an equivalent form of the parallel postulate. It states:

Given a line and a point not on the line, there is exactly one line parallel to the given line passing through the point.

This theorem simplifies the fifth postulate of Euclid into a more intuitive and practical form, often used in modern geometry.

Explanation:

- The theorem asserts the uniqueness of the parallel line through a given point.

- It ensures that for any line l and point P not on l, only one line m can be drawn through P such that $m \parallel l$.

- This property is central to Euclidean geometry and does not hold in non-Euclidean geometries like hyperbolic or spherical geometry.

Example in Action:

- Consider a line l and a point P not on l. Using Playfair's Theorem, you can draw a unique line m through P that never intersects l, regardless of how far the lines are extended.

- In a coordinate system, if l has the equation $y = mx + b$ and $P(x_1, y_1)$ is a point, the equation of the parallel line through P is $y = mx + c$, where c is determined by substituting (x_1, y_1).

Topic 4
Congruent Triangles

4.1 Basic Classification of Triangles 76
4.2 Congruent Triangles 78
4.3 Congruence Postulates 80
4.4 Finding Congruent Triangles in Isosceles Triangle 81

4.1 Basic Classification of Triangles

1. We can classify triangles by *side lengths*.

    [1] scalene triangle : all side lengths are distinct.

    [2] isosceles : two side lengths are equal.

    [3] equilateral : all side lengths are equal.

2. We can classify triangles by *angle measures*.

    [1] acute triangle : all angle measures are acute.

    [2] right : one of the angle is right angle.

    [3] obtuse : one of the angle is obtuse angle.

    [4] equiangular : all angle measures are equal.

For angles, we can divide angles into two kinds : interior and exterior. Interior angles are the given angles inside a triangle. On the other hand, exterior angles are angles that form a linear pair with interior angles.

It is important to draw an auxiliary line, which is useful and sometimes necessary to prove the theorems we are about to see. Use this with the uniqueness of parallel line postulates.

Now, we lay out the sum of interior angles of triangle theorem and the exterior angle theorem, all of which can be proved by drawing a parallel line to $\overline{AD}$ that passes through B.

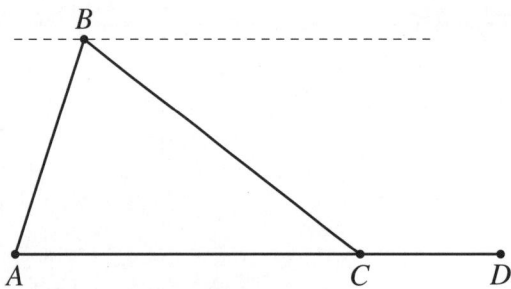

Given a triangle ABC, the sum of interior angles is $180°$, which makes the measure of exterior angle the sum of measures of non-adjacent interior angles, which are known as *remote interior angles*.

> **Sum of Interior Angles of Triangle Theorem(or Triangle Angle Sum Theorem)**
> *The sum of interior angles of any non-degenerate triangle is $180°$.*

> **Exterior Angle Theorem**
> *The sum of two remote interior angles equals the measure of an exterior angle.*

Example 34

Classify a triangle ABC by side lengths where $AB = 4$, $BC = 4$, and $AC = 6$.

Example 35

Classify a triangle DEF by side lengths where $AB = 3$, $BC = 4$, and $AC = 5$.

Example 36

Classify a triangle ABC by angle measures where $AB = 5$, $BC = 12$, and $AC = 13$.

Example 37

Given a triangle ABC where $m\angle A = 40°$, $m\angle B = 70°$, compute the measure of $\angle C$.

Here is the solution to the problems written above.

Example 34. Triangle ABC is isosceles.

Example 35. Triangle DEF is scalene.

Example 36. Triangle ABC is right.

Example 37. $m\angle C = 180° - 40° - 70° = 70°$.

4.2 Congruent Triangles

Triangles are congruent if they have the same size and shape. This is also known as *CPCTC*, which stands for *corresponding parts of congruent triangles are congruent*. The following figure shows that $\triangle ABC$ is congruent to $\triangle DEF$.

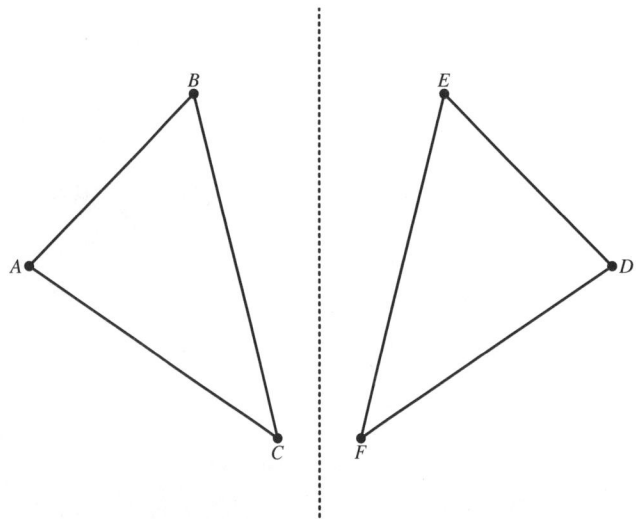

- Triangle congruence is "reflexive." : $\triangle ABC \cong \triangle ABC$.

- Triangle congruence is "symmetric." : if $\triangle ABC \cong \triangle DEF$, then $\triangle DEF \cong \triangle ABC$.

- Triangle congruence is "transitive." : if $\triangle ABC \cong \triangle DEF$, then $\triangle DEF \cong \triangle PQR$, then $\triangle ABC \cong \triangle PQR$.

There are three transformations preserving congruence relationship between triangles.

- Translation : it is sometimes known as *slide*.

- Reflection : it is sometimes known as *flip*.

- Rotation : it is known as *turn* or *spin*.

> **CPCTC**
> *Corresponding parts of congruent triangles are congruent.*

In particular, if two congruent triangles are given, then their corresponding parts are all equivalent, respectively, thanks to CPCTC. On the other hand, if their corresponding parts are all equivalent, without any reference to their congruence relationships, we conclude that the triangles must be congruent to one another, due to CPCTC.

Example 38

Given a triangle ABC where $A = (2,0), B = (0,2), C = (-2,0)$, find the coordinates of a triangle $A'B'C'$, the image of reflection of $\triangle ABC$ about the line $y = -1$.

Example 39

Given a triangle ABC where $A = (2,0), B = (0,2), C = (-2,0)$, rotate it about the point B counterclockwise $90°$. Find all the coordinates of the resulting triangle.

Example 40

Given a triangle ABC where $A = (2,0), B = (0,2), C = (-2,0)$, translate all vertices by a vector $<3,4>$. Here, a vector $<3,4>$ means the transformation directed by 3 units right and 4 units up. Find the coordinates of the resulting triangle.

Here is the solution to the examples covered above.

Example 38. Since *flip* uses the line of symmetry, by using the property of midpoint, we get $A' = (2,-2), B' = (0,-4), C' = (-2,-2)$.

Example 39. Perform rotation directly to the figure. We find out that B stays unchanged, whereas A goes to $(2,4)$, and C goes to $(2,0)$.

Example 40. $A(2,0)$ goes to $(5,4)$. $B(0,2)$ goes to $(3,6)$. Finally, $C(-2,0)$ goes to $(1,4)$.

4.3 Congruence Postulates

Applying CPCTC every time would be inefficient, so mathematicians came up with some basic postulates we could use for proving triangle congruence. There are three main postulates one may use in proving theorems about triangle congruence.

(1) SSS-congruence : If three sides are congruent to the corresponding sides, then the two triangles are congruent.

(2) SAS-congruence : If two sides and an included angle are congruent to the corresponding sides and angle, then the two are congruent.

(3) ASA-congruence : If two angles and the included side are congruent to the corresponding angles and the side, then the two are congruent.

Example 41

From the example 38, a triangle $A'B'C'$ is a reflection of ABC where $A = (2,0), B = (0,2), C = (-2,0)$. What postulate can be applied to show that they are congruent?

Example 42

Given two triangles $\triangle ABC$ and $\triangle DEF$ where $AB = DE$ and $AC = DF$ and $\angle A \cong \angle D$, apply one of the postulates to show that the two are congruent.

Here is the solution to the examples covered above.

Example 41. Since $A' = (2,-2), B' = (0,-4), C' = (-2,-2)$ for $\triangle A'B'C'$ and $A = (2,0), B = (0,2), C = (-2,0)$ for $\triangle ABC$, there is no reference of angle whatsoever. On the other hand, we can easily find out $A'B' = AB, A'C' = AC, B'C' = BC$. Therefore, by SSS congruence, $\triangle ABC$ and $\triangle A'B'C'$ are congruent.

Example 42. This is a direct application of SAS congruence postulate.

4.4 Finding Congruent Triangles in Isosceles Triangle

When you see a point off the line segment, it is handy and useful if we find a perpendicular foot on that line segment. The angle formed by the congruent sides is the *vertex angle*. The other two angles are called the *base angles*. The following figure shows that the perpendicular bisector of the base side is not different from the angle bisector of the vertex angle for an isosceles triangle.

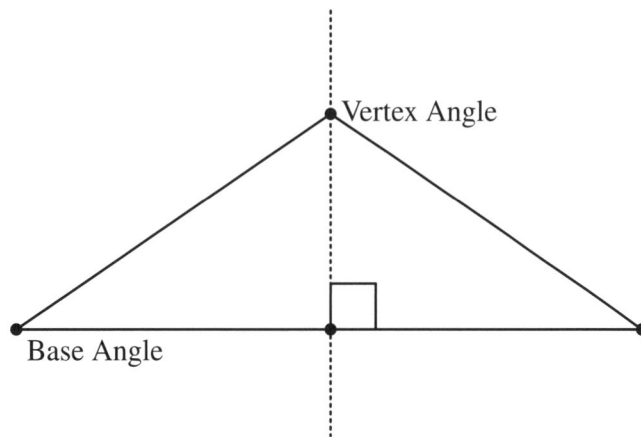

There are two theorems we should know to prove theorems related to isosceles triangles, the proofs of which will be covered in detail in walk-through practices.

Isosceles Triangle Theorem
Given a triangle, if two sides are congruent, then two corresponding angles are congruent.

Converse of Isosceles Triangle Theorem
Given a triangle, if two angles are congruent, then two corresponding sides are congruent.

IT theorem and Converse of IT theorem can be proved by using HA congruence or HL congruence theorems. These theorems suggest that if two angles of a triangle are congruent, then corresponding sides are congruent, and vice versa.

Also, notice that any isosceles triangle has such property that its perpendicular bisector of the base is congruent to the angle bisector of the vertex angle. We use this multiple times to find heights in problem-solving classes.

Drawing a perpendicular bisector shows the purpose of using Pythagorean Theorem, and isosceles triangles generally show such pattern of concept application. Have a close look at the examples in the next page.

Example 43

Determine whether $\triangle ABC$ where $A = (1,3), B = (0,6), C = (-1,3)$ is an isosceles triangle.

Example 44

Given a triangle ABC where $AB = BC$, if $m\angle B = 40°$, determine the measure of $\angle A$.

Example 45

Given a triangle ABC where $AB = 10$, $BC = 10$ and $AC = 16$, find the area of the triangle.

Here is the solution to the examples covered above.

Example 43. By computing AB, BC, AC, we get $AB = BC = \sqrt{10} \neq AC$. Therefore, $\triangle ABC$ is isosceles.

Example 44. Since $m\angle A = m\angle C$, by IT theorem, we may use SIAT(sum of interior angles of triangle) theorem to conclude that $m\angle A = 70°$.

Example 45. The triangle is isosceles, so drop the altitude from B to $\overline{AC}$. The angle bisector and perpendicular bisector imply that the altitude cuts $\overline{AC}$ into half. Hence, applying Pythagorean Theorem, we get the height 6. Thus, the area of ABC equals 48.

Walk-Through Practices

47. Find the measure of sides $\triangle ABC$, if $A = (0,2)$, $B = (2,1)$, and $C = (1,4)$. Classify the triangle by sides.

48. Some textbooks call this a postulate. Here, we consider it as a theorem. Prove that the sum of interior angles of a triangle is $180°$.

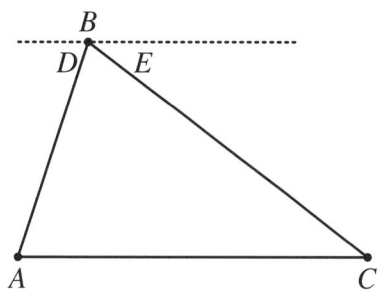

Statement	Reason
1. Transversal is parallel to $\overline{AC}$. D, B, and E form a straight angle.	1. Given
2. $\angle A \cong \angle D$. $\angle C \cong \angle E$.	2.
3. $m\angle A = m\angle D$. $m\angle C = m\angle E$.	3.
4. $m\angle D + m\angle B + m\angle E = 180°$.	4.
5. $m\angle A + m\angle B + m\angle C = 180°$.	5.

49. Prove that the measure of exterior angle of a triangle is the sum of measures of non-adjacent interior angles.

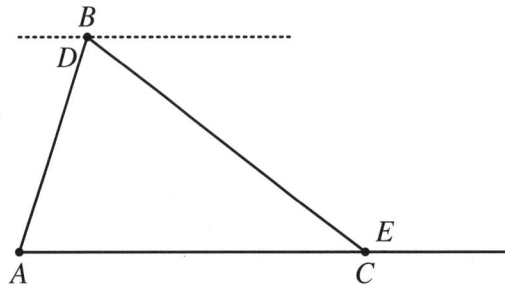

Statement	Reason
1. Transversal is parallel to $\overline{AC}$.	1. Given
2. $\angle D \cong \angle A$.	2. Alternate Interior Angle Theorem
3. $m\angle D = m\angle A$.	3.
4. $m\angle D + m\angle B = m\angle E$.	4. Alternate Interior Angle Theorem
5. $m\angle A + m\angle B = m\angle E$.	5.

50. If $\overline{TU} \perp \overline{UV}$ and $\overline{UV} \perp \overline{VW}$, find $m\angle X$.

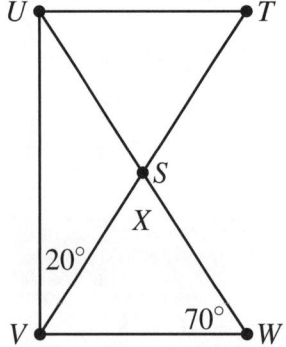

51. Prove that if $\triangle ABC \cong \triangle DEF$ and $\triangle DEF \cong \triangle XYZ$, then $\triangle ABC \cong \triangle XYZ$.

Statement	Reason
1. $\triangle ABC \cong \triangle DEF$. $\triangle DEF \cong \triangle XYZ$	1. Given
2. $\angle A \cong \angle D$. $\angle B \cong \angle E$. $\angle C \cong \angle F$. $\overline{AB} \cong \overline{DE}$. $\overline{BC} \cong \overline{EF}$. $\overline{AC} \cong \overline{DF}$.	2.
3. $\angle X \cong \angle D$. $\angle Y \cong \angle E$. $\angle Z \cong \angle F$. $\overline{XY} \cong \overline{DE}$. $\overline{YZ} \cong \overline{EF}$. $\overline{XZ} \cong \overline{DF}$.	3.
4. $\angle X \cong \angle A$. $\angle Y \cong \angle B$. $\angle Z \cong \angle C$. $\overline{XY} \cong \overline{AB}$. $\overline{YZ} \cong \overline{BC}$. $\overline{XZ} \cong \overline{AC}$.	4.
5. $\triangle ABC \cong \triangle XYZ$.	5.

52. Determine whether $\triangle ABC \cong \triangle DEF$ where $A = (4,0), B = (2,2), C = (3,-1)$ and $D = (-2,0), E = (-1,1), F = (0,-1)$.

53. Given two right triangles, if hypotenuse is congruent to the corresponding side, and one of the legs is congruent to the corresponding side, then prove that the two triangles are congruent. In particular, let $\triangle ABC$ and $\triangle DEF$ be right triangles with $\angle B$ and $\angle E$ be the right angles, and assume that $\overline{AC} \cong \overline{DF}$ and $\overline{AB} \cong \overline{DE}$. (This is the proof of HL congruence theorem.)

Statement	Reason
1. $\overline{AC} \cong \overline{DF}$. $\overline{AB} \cong \overline{DE}$. $\angle B$ and $\angle E$ are right angles.	1. Given
2. $AC = DF$. $AB = DE$.	2.
3. $AB^2 + BC^2 = AC^2$. $DE^2 + EF^2 = DF^2$	3. Pythagorean Theorem
4. $AB^2 + BC^2 = DF^2$.	4.
5. $AB^2 + BC^2 = DE^2 + EF^2$.	5.
6. $DE^2 + BC^2 = DE^2 + EF^2$.	6.
7. $BC^2 = EF^2$. (Hence, $BC = EF$ by zero-product property.)	7.
8. $\triangle ABC \cong \triangle DEF$.	8.

54. If two angles and non-included side are congruent to the corresponding angles and side, then the two triangles are congruent. In particular, let $\triangle ABC$ and $\triangle DEF$ be the two. Assume that $\angle A \cong \angle D$, $\angle B \cong \angle E$, and $\overline{BC} \cong \overline{EF}$, without loss of generality. (This is the proof of AAS congruence theorem.)

Statement	Reason
1. $\angle A \cong \angle D$. $\angle B \cong \angle E$. $\overline{BC} \cong \overline{EF}$	1. Given
2. $m\angle A + m\angle B + m\angle C = 180°$. $m\angle D + m\angle E + m\angle F = 180°$.	2. Sum of Interior Angles of Triangle Theorem
3. $m\angle A + m\angle B + m\angle C = m\angle D + m\angle E + m\angle F$.	3.
4. $m\angle A = m\angle D$. $m\angle B = m\angle E$.	4.
5. $m\angle A + m\angle B + m\angle C = m\angle A + m\angle B + m\angle F$.	5.
6. $m\angle C = m\angle F$.	6.
7. $\angle C \cong \angle F$.	7.
8. $\triangle ABC \cong \triangle DEF$.	8.

55. Given two right triangles, if an angle and a leg are congruent to the corresponding angle and leg, then the two right triangles are congruent. In particular, let $\triangle ABC$ and $\triangle DEF$ be right triangles with $\angle B$ and $\angle E$ be the right angles, and assume that $\overline{AB} \cong \overline{DE}$ and $\angle A \cong \angle D$. (This is the proof of AL congruence theorem.)

Statement	Reason
1. $\overline{AB} \cong \overline{DE}$. $\angle A \cong \angle D$. $\angle B$ and $\angle E$ are right angles.	1. Given
2. $AB = DE$.	2.
3. $m\angle A = m\angle D$.	3.
4. $m\angle B = 90°$. $m\angle E = 90°$.	4.
5. $m\angle B = m\angle E$.	5.
6. $\triangle ABC \cong \triangle DEF$.	6.

56. Given two right triangles, if two legs are congruent to the corresponding legs, then the two right triangles are congruent. In particular, let $\triangle ABC$ and $\triangle DEF$ be right triangles with $\angle B$ and $\angle E$ be the right angles. Assume that $\overline{AB} \cong \overline{DE}$ and $\overline{BC} \cong \overline{EF}$. (Remark: one may prove this using either SSS or SAS congruence postulate.)

Statement	Reason
1. $\overline{AB} \cong \overline{DE}$. $\overline{BC} \cong \overline{EF}$. $\angle B$ and $\angle E$ are right angles.	1. Given
2. $AB = DE$. $BC = EF$.	2.
3. $m\angle B = 90°$. $m\angle E = 90°$.	3.
4. $m\angle B = m\angle E$.	4.
5. $\triangle ABC \cong \triangle DEF$.	5.

57. Given two right triangles, if the hypotenuse and an angle are congruent to the corresponding hypotenuse and the angle, then the two triangles are congruent. In particular, let $\triangle ABC$ and $\triangle DEF$ be right triangles with B and E be the right angles. Assume that $\overline{AC} \cong \overline{DF}$ and $\angle A \cong \angle D$, without loss of generality.

Statement	Reason
1. $\overline{AC} \cong \overline{DF}$. $\angle A \cong \angle D$. $\angle B$ and $\angle E$ are right angles.	1. Given
2. $AC = DF$.	2.
3. $m\angle A = m\angle D$.	3.
4. $m\angle B = 90°$. $m\angle E = 90°$.	4.
5. $m\angle B = m\angle E$.	5.
6. $\triangle ABC \cong \triangle DEF$.	6.

58. If $\overline{DF}$ bisects $\angle CDE$ where F is on $\overline{CE}$, and $\overline{CE} \perp \overline{DF}$, then prove $\triangle DFC \cong \triangle DFE$.

Statement	Reason
1. $\overline{DF}$ bisects $\angle CDE$. $\overline{CE} \perp \overline{DF}$.	1. Given
2. $\angle FDC \cong \angle FDE$.	2. Definition of Angle Bisector
3. $\angle CFD$ and $\angle EFD$ are right angles.	3.
4. $\overline{DF} \cong \overline{DF}$.	4.
5. $\triangle DFC \cong \triangle DFE$.	5.

59. If a triangle is isosceles, then the base angles are congruent. This is the proof of isosceles triangle theorem. Let △ABC be isosceles such that $\overline{AB}$ and $\overline{AC}$ are congruent by assumption. Let D be the point on $\overline{BC}$ such that $\overline{AD}$ is perpendicular to $\overline{BC}$.

Statement	Reason
1. $\overline{AB} \cong \overline{AC}$. $\overline{AD} \perp \overline{BC}$.	1. Given
2. $AB = AC$.	2.
3. ∠ADB and ∠ADC are right angles.	3.
4. $\overline{AD} \cong \overline{AD}$.	4.
5. $AD = AD$.	5.
6. △ABD ≅ △ACD.	6.
7. ∠B ≅ ∠C.	7.

60. If two angles are congruent, then the sides opposite these angles are congruent. Let △ABC be isosceles such that ∠B and ∠C are congruent by assumption. Let D be the point on $\overline{BC}$ such that $\overline{AD}$ is perpendicular to $\overline{BC}$.

Statement	Reason
1. ∠B ≅ ∠C. $\overline{AD} \perp \overline{BC}$.	1. Given
2. $m\angle B = m\angle C$.	2.
3. ∠ADB and ∠ADC are right angles.	3.
4. $\overline{AD} \cong \overline{AD}$.	4.
5. $AD = AD$.	5.
6. △ABD ≅ △ACD.	6.
7. $AB = AC$.	7.

61. In the diagram, $AC = CD = DB$ where $m\angle B = 30°$. Find $m\angle A$. Notice that the figure is not drawn to scale.

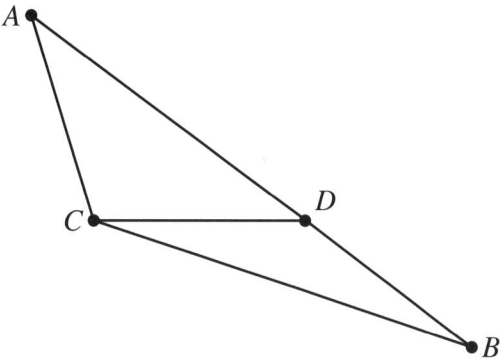

62. In the diagram, $AB = AC = 10$ and $m\angle A = 60°$. Find BC.

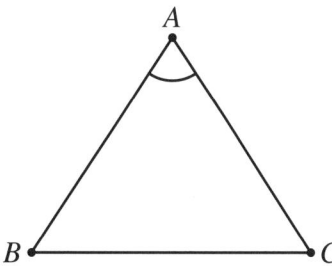

63. Given an isosceles triangle △ABC where $AB = AC$, if $AD = BD = BC$, find the measure of ∠A.

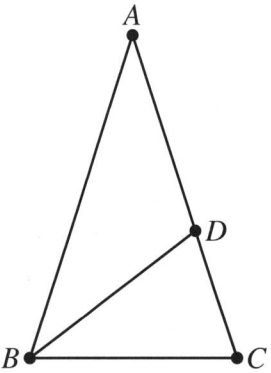

Skill Practice

Problem 1
Given a triangle ABC, if $m\angle A = 45°$, $m\angle B = 65°$, then determine the measure of $\angle C$, in degrees, in accordance with *Sum of Interior Angles of Triangle Theorem*.

Problem 2
Determine the sum of all base angles of a right isosceles triangle.

Problem 3
Determine the vertex angle measure of an isosceles triangle whose base angle has the measure of $30°$.

Problem 4
Determine the measure of an exterior angle of an equilateral triangle.

Problem 5
Classify a triangle ABC by angle measures where $AB = 8$, $BC = 15$, and $AC = 17$. (Apply Pythagorean Theorem.)

Problem 6
Given a right triangle ABC where $\angle B$ is right, if $AC = 25$, $BC = 24$, determine the exact value of AB.

Problem 7
Given an isosceles triangle ABC, if $m\angle A = 120°$, $m\angle B = 30°$, then determine the measure of $m\angle C$, in degrees.

Problem 8
According to the exterior angle theorem, if $m\angle A = 30°$, $m\angle B = 45°$, then determine the measure of exterior angle of $\angle C$, in degrees.

Problem 9
Given an isosceles triangle $\triangle ABC$, where $AB = BC$, if $m\angle A = 70$, then determine the measure of $m\angle C$, according to *Isosceles Triangle Theorem*.

Problem 10
Given a triangle $\triangle ABC$, where $m\angle A = m\angle C = 80°$, if $AB = 10$, then determine the measure of BC, according to *Converse of Isosceles Triangle Theorem*.

Answer Key

1. 70°

2. 90°

3. 120°

4. 120°

5. Right triangle

6. 7

7. 30°

8. 75°

9. 70

10. 10

BEFORE YOU MOVE ON

The Golden Ratio

Definition: The Golden Ratio, often denoted by the Greek letter ϕ (phi), is a special mathematical constant that occurs when a line is divided into two parts such that the ratio of the whole line to the larger part is the same as the ratio of the larger part to the smaller part. Mathematically, this is expressed as:

$$\phi = \frac{1+\sqrt{5}}{2} \approx 1.618.$$

The Golden Ratio appears in art, architecture, nature, and mathematics due to its aesthetically pleasing properties.

Mathematical Expression:

- If a line segment is divided into two parts, a (the larger part) and b (the smaller part), the Golden Ratio satisfies:

$$\frac{a+b}{a} = \frac{a}{b} = \phi.$$

- Solving this equation yields $\phi = \dfrac{1+\sqrt{5}}{2}$.

Fun Fact: The Golden Ratio is sometimes called the "Divine Proportion" because of its unique and ubiquitous presence in the natural world and its perceived perfection in design and structure.

Topic 5
Triangle Properties

5.1 Angle Bisector Theorem 96
5.2 Points of Concurrency 98
5.3 Properties of Right Triangle 101
5.4 Triangular Inequality 102

5.1 Angle Bisector Theorem

First, if there is a point P and a line l that does not contain P, we can always draw a parallel line to the line or a perpendicular line to it. When we draw a perpendicular line segment to the line, we get the altitude. This idea will show the angle bisector theorem.

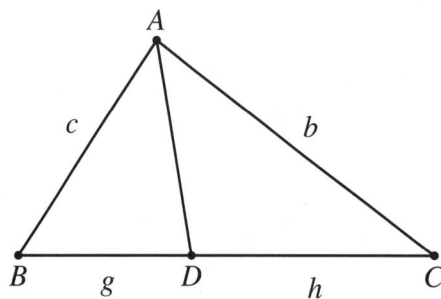

The angle bisector theorem states that if $\overline{AD}$ is the angle bisector of $\angle A$, then we get the ratio equation

$$\frac{AB}{AC} = \frac{BD}{CD}$$

This is true because of the property of angle bisector. Look at the following figure to understand why this must be true. Follow the procedures and see what happens.

1. Drop an altitude from D to $\overline{AB}$. Call its length h', read as h prime. Likewise, drop an altitude from D to $\overline{AC}$. Its length equals h'. Think about why this is true.

2. Find the area of $\triangle ABD$ and $\triangle ACD$. In particular, $[ABD] = \frac{1}{2} \times c \times h'$. Likewise, $[ACD] = \frac{1}{2} \times b \times h'$. Find the ratio between $[ABD]$ and $[ACD]$.

3. Drop an altitude from A to $\overline{BC}$. Call its length H.

4. Check that $[ABD] = \frac{1}{2} \times g \times H$. Likewise, $[ACD] = \frac{1}{2} \times h \times H$. Find the ratio between $[ABD]$ and $[ACD]$.

Remark

fixed heights $\implies$ area ratio = base ratio

fixed bases $\implies$ area ratio = height ratio

Example 46

Given a triangle ABC where $AB = 5$, $BC = 12$, and $AC = 13$, let D be the point on $\overline{AC}$ such that $\overline{BD}$ is the angle bisector of $\angle ABC$. Find AD.

Example 47

Given a triangle ABC where $AB = 3$, $BC = 4$, and $AC = 5$, let D be the point on $\overline{AC}$ such that $\overline{BD}$ is the angle bisector of $\angle ABC$. Find $AD : CD$.

Example 48

Given a triangle ABC where $AB = 13$, $BC = 14$, and $AC = 15$, the angle bisector of $\angle BAC$ cuts $\overline{BC}$ into two segments of different lengths. Find the lengths of these segments.

Here is the solution to the examples covered above.

Example 46. $AD : CD = 5 : 12$, so $AD = 5k$ and $CD = 12k$. Hence, $AD + CD = 17k = 13$. This implies that $k = \dfrac{13}{17}$. Hence, $AD = \dfrac{65}{17}$.

Example 47. According to the angle bisector theorem, $AD : CD = 3 : 4$.

Example 48. According to the angle bisector theorem, the two segments are cut into the ratio of 13 and 15. Hence, $13k + 15k = 14$ implies that $k = 0.5$. The segments have lengths of 6.5 and 7.5.

Topic_1 Basic Elements of Geometry

5.2 Points of Concurrency

5.2.1 Circumcenter

The perpendicular bisectors of the sides of a triangle are concurrent at a point called the circumcenter. The circle centered at the circumcenter that passes through the vertices of the original triangle is called the circumcircle of the triangle because it is circumscribed about the triangle (meaning it passes through all the vertices of the triangle).

Finally, the radius of this circle is called the circumradius, the circumcenter is usually labeled with the letter O, and the circumradius is usually called R.

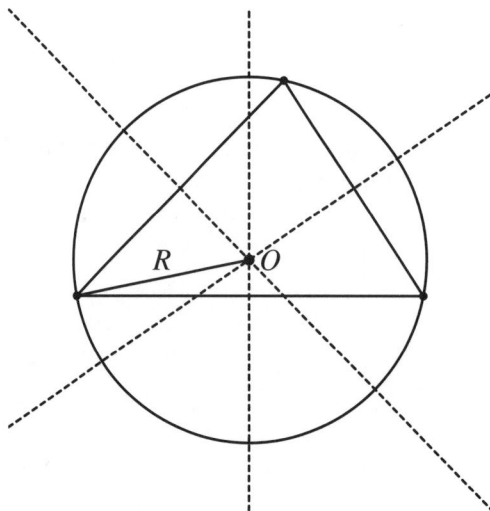

5.2.2 Incenter

The angle bisectors of a triangle are concurrent at a point called the incenter. This point is equidistant from the sides of the triangle. This common distance from the incenter to the sides of a triangle is called the inradius, because the circle with center I and this radius is tangent to all three sides of the triangle. This circle is unsurprisingly called the incircle because it is inscribed in the triangle (meaning it is tangent to all the sides of the triangle). The incenter is usually denoted I, and the inradius is usually written as r.

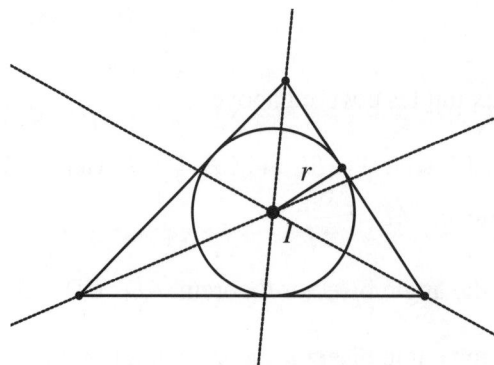

5.2.3 Centroid

A median of a triangle connects a vertex of a triangle to the midpoint of the opposite side. The medians of a triangle are concurrent at a point called the centroid of the triangle. The centroid of the triangle is usually labeled G.

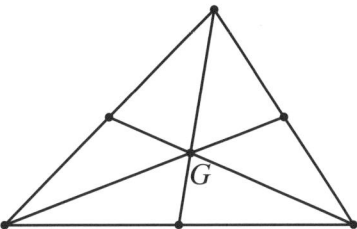

1. The medians of a triangle partition the triangle into six triangles of same area.

2. The centroid of a triangle cuts the medians into 2 : 1 ratio.

5.2.4 Orthocenter

The altitudes of a triangle (extended if necessary) are concurrent at the orthocenter of the triangle, which is usually denoted H.

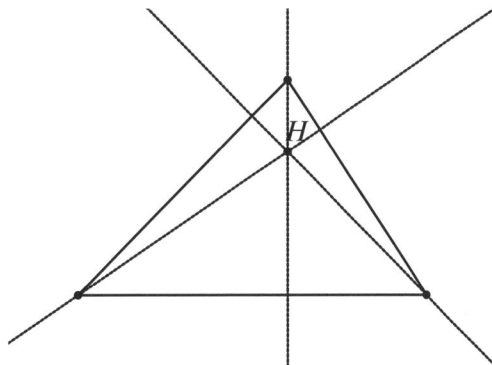

1. The orthocenter of an acute triangle is inside the triangle.

2. The orthocenter of a right triangle is the vertex of the right angle.

3. The orthocenter of an obtuse triangle is outside the triangle.

Example 49

Find the circumradius of an equilateral triangle with the side length of 6.

Example 50

Find the inradius of the triangle whose side lengths are 7, 24, and 25.

Here is the solution to the examples covered above.

Example 49. Using Pythagorean Theorem, one should solve $R^2 = (3\sqrt{3} - R)^2 + 3^2$ to retrieve $R = 2\sqrt{3}$.

Example 50. Use the formula $sr = 84$, where $s = \dfrac{7+24+25}{2} = 28$. Hence, $r = \dfrac{84}{28} = 3$.

100   The Essential Guide to Geometry

5.3 Properties of Right Triangle

In any right triangle, the sum of the squares of the legs equals the square of the hypotenuse. For a right triangle with side lengths $a \leq b \leq c$, then it is true that

$$a^2 + b^2 = c^2.$$

This is the famous Pythagorean Theorem. We will prove this after learning similar triangles. This section covers its application.

There are two special right triangles, which are known as

- $45 - 45 - 90$ triangle : it is also known as the right isosceles triangle.
- $30 - 60 - 90$ triangle : it is the most commonly used right triangle.

Other than special right triangles, we may have to find whether the given triangle is a right triangle by simply looking at its side lengths.

The next thing we should learn is called Pythagorean Triple, and it may be useful if we apply the following formula

$$(2n)^2 + (n^2 - 1)^2 = (n^2 + 1)^2$$

for a triangle with side length triple $(2n, n^2 - 1, n^2 + 1)$. There are infinitely many triples, including $(3,4,5)$, $(5,12,13)$, $(7,24,25)$, and $(8,15,17)$.

Example 51

Determine whether 39, 52 and 65 form a right triangle.

Example 52

Inscribed in a circle is a quadrilateral having side lengths of $10, 24, 13\sqrt{2}, 13\sqrt{2}$, consecutively. What is the radius of the circle?

Here is the solution of examples covered above.

Example 51. Since $39 : 52 : 65 = 3 : 4 : 5$, we get a Pythagorean triple, so it is a right triangle.

Example 52. Notice that $10, 24, 26$ form a right triangle by one of the Pythagorean triples $(5, 12, 13)$. Also, $13\sqrt{2}, 13\sqrt{2}, 26$ form a right triangle by $(1 : 1 : \sqrt{2})$. Hence, we get the diameter of 26, which implies that the radius is 13.

5.4 Triangular Inequality

First, in any triangle, the longest side is opposite the largest angle and the shortest side is opposite the smallest angle. The middle side, of course, is opposite part of the middle angle.

> **Angle-Side Theorem** or Side-Angle Theorem
> Given a $\triangle ABC$, $AB \geq AC \geq BC$ if and only if $m\angle C \geq m\angle B \geq m\angle A$.

This means that angle opposite to side are somewhat proportional. The special case is called the *Base Angle Theorem*. It states that in an isosceles triangle, the angles opposite the congruent sides are congruent.

Second, Pythagorean Theorem is not just used for a right triangle. It may address the problem of whether a given triangle is a right one or not. This is useful when we have an integer-value triangle whose side lengths are not familiar numbers.

1. $\angle C$ of $\triangle ABC$ is acute if and only if $AB^2 < AC^2 + BC^2$.
2. $\angle C$ of $\triangle ABC$ is right if and only if $AB^2 = AC^2 + BC^2$.
3. $\angle C$ of $\triangle ABC$ is obtuse if and only if $AB^2 > AC^2 + BC^2$.

Third, there is a triangular inequality states that any side of a triangle must be smaller than the sum of the other two.

> **Triangular Inequality**
> For any three points, A, B, and C, we have
> $$AB + BC \geq AC,$$
> where equality holds if and only if B is on $\overline{AC}$.

Therefore, for non-degenerate triangles (i.e., those in which the vertices are not collinear), $AB + BC > AC$.

Example 53

What are the possible values of x for $x, 4, 8$ to be a triangle?

Here is the solution to the example covered above.

Example 53. If x is not the longest side, then $x + 4 > 8$. Therefore, $x > 4$. On the other hand, if x is the longest side, then $x < 4 + 8 = 12$. Therefore, any real number between 4 and 12 will suffice.

Walk-Through Practices

64. If $m\angle B = 90°$ and D is the point of intersection between the angle bisector of $\angle A$ and $\overline{BC}$, find the area of $\triangle ADC$.

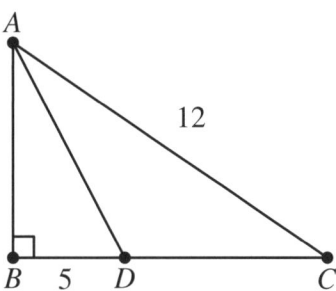

65. If $BD = 6, DA = 8, BC = 2x+1$ and $AC = 3x-5$, find the length of $\overline{AC}$. (Notice that the figure is not drawn to scale. Reason why x is a valid value, using Triangular Inequality.)

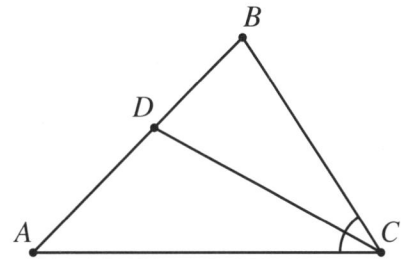

Topic_1 Basic Elements of Geometry

66. Find the circumradius of an equilateral triangle with side length 10.

67. Find the length of the inradius of a triangle whose side lengths are 6, 8, 10.

68. Medians $\overline{AX}$ and $\overline{BY}$ of $\triangle ABC$ have the same length. Prove that $AC = BC$.

69. Given a triangle $\triangle ABC$, altitudes $\overline{CD}$ and $\overline{BE}$ intersect at F. Given that $m\angle ABC = 70°$ and $m\angle BCA = 45°$, find $m\angle FAC$. (Figure is not drawn to scale.)

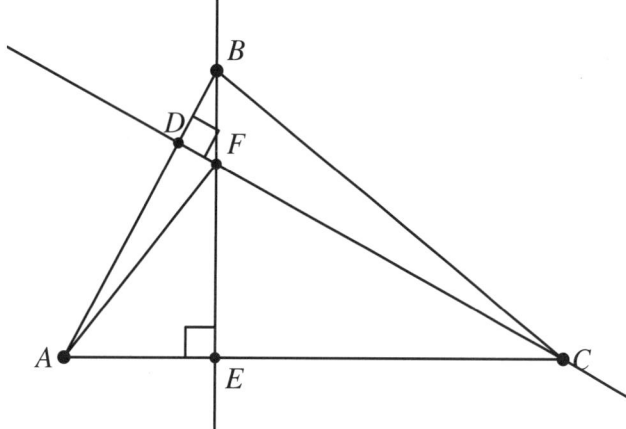

70. Given $AB = BC = 13$ and $AC = 10$, find the circumradius of $\triangle ABC$.

71. Assume that D, E, and F are points of tangency to the incircle. If $AB = 13$cm, $BC = 15$cm, $CA = 8$cm, find AF.

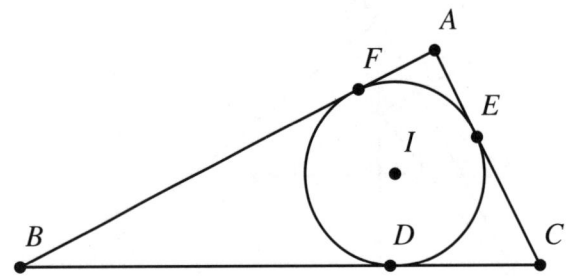

72. Find the area of an equilateral triangle with side length 6.

73. In $\triangle ABC$, if $AB = 30$, $m\angle A = 30°$, and $m\angle C = 45°$, find the area of triangle ABC.

74. Assume that $\overline{BC}$ is the base of isosceles triangle $\triangle ABC$. Given that $BC > AB$, show that $m\angle A > 60°$.

75. How many different obtuse triangles with integer side lengths with the perimeter of 20 can we draw such that no two of them is congruent?

76. The length of each leg of an isosceles triangle is $x+1$ and the length of the base is $3x-2$. Determine all possible integer values of x.

Solutions to walk-through practices can be found in the solution manual. Go to page 225.

Skill Practice

Problem 1
Given an isosceles triangle ABC where $AB = BC$, if $AB = 4$, determine the possible number of integer values of AC.

Problem 2
Evaluate the area of triangle whose side lengths are 13, 14, and 15.

Problem 3
Evaluate the area of triangle whose side lengths are 10, 10 and 16.

Problem 4
Evaluate the length of inradius for triangle whose side lengths are 13, 14 and 15.

Problem 5
If the area of triangle, whose side lengths are unknown, is 20, and the length of inradius is 4, determine its perimeter.

Problem 6
Determine the circumradius of an equilateral triangle whose side length equals 10.

Problem 7
Determine the length of circumradius of a right triangle whose side lengths are 7, 24, and 25.

Problem 8
Determine the circumference of circumcircle of a right triangle whose side lengths are 8, 15, and 17.

Problem 9
If the length of the median of an equilateral triangle equals $20\sqrt{3}$, determine the value of its perimeter.

Problem 10
According to the angle-bisector theorem, if $AB : BC = 5 : 7$, the angle bisector from B to $\overline{AC}$ cuts $\overline{AC}$ into segments of length ratio $a : b$. If a and b are relatively prime, determine $a + b$.

STEWART'S THEOREM

Stewart's Theorem is a classical result in geometry that relates the lengths of the sides of a triangle to a ceviana segment drawn from a vertex to the opposite side (or its extension). This theorem provides a convenient formula for solving problems involving cevians in triangles.

Consider a triangle $\triangle ABC$ with a cevian AD, where D divides side BC into segments BD and DC. Let:

$$AB = c, \quad AC = b, \quad BC = a, \quad BD = m, \quad DC = n, \quad AD = d.$$

Stewart's Theorem states that the following equation holds:

$$m \cdot a \cdot n + d \cdot a \cdot d = b \cdot m \cdot b + c \cdot n \cdot c,$$

where $m + n = a$.

This theorem is particularly useful in problems where the cevian splits the triangle into segments, allowing the relationship between the lengths to be computed efficiently. It bridges geometry with algebra, making it a powerful tool for problem-solving in competition mathematics and analytical geometry.

Answer Key

1. 7

2. 84

3. 48

4. 4

5. 10

6. $\dfrac{10\sqrt{3}}{3}$

7. $\dfrac{25}{2}$ or 12.5

8. 17π

9. 120

10. 12

BEFORE YOU MOVE ON

Menelaus' Theorem

Statement of the Theorem: Menelaus' Theorem is a fundamental result in geometry that establishes a relationship between the ratios of segments created when a transversal intersects the sides of a triangle (or their extensions).

Let $\triangle ABC$ be a triangle, and let a transversal line intersect BC, CA, and AB at points D, E, and F, respectively. Menelaus' Theorem states:

$$\frac{BD}{DC} \cdot \frac{CE}{EA} \cdot \frac{AF}{FB} = 1.$$

Explanation:

- The theorem applies when the points D, E, F are collinear.

- The segments BD, DC, CE, EA, AF, FB can represent directed distances, making the theorem valid even when the transversal crosses the triangle externally.

- Menelaus' Theorem provides a condition for the collinearity of the points D, E, F.

Historical Note: Named after the Greek mathematician Menelaus of Alexandria, this theorem dates back to the 1st century AD and has been instrumental in the development of projective geometry.

Topic 6
Similar Triangles

6.1 Similar Triangles 116

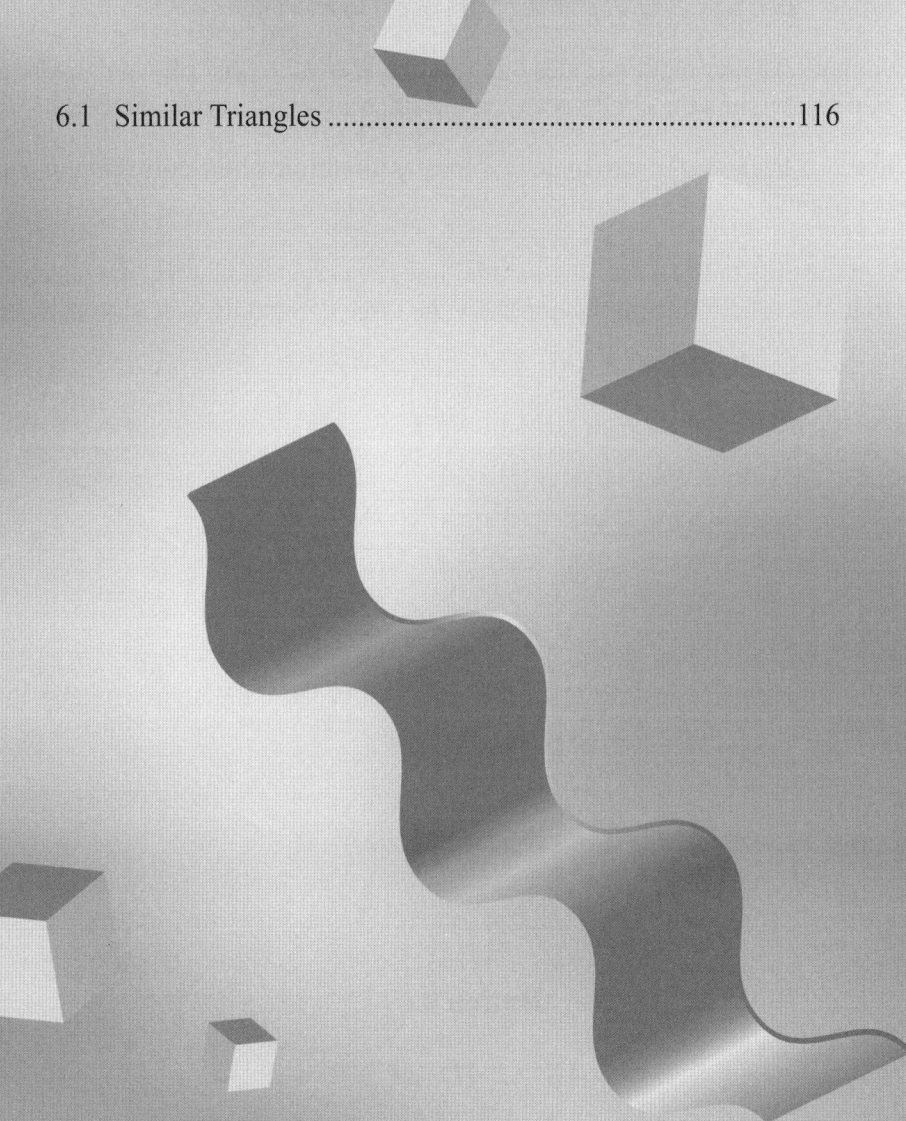

6.1 Similar Triangles

We say two figures are *similar* if one is simply a scaled version of the other, including a possible rotation or reflection of it.

(1) Corresponding angles in similar figures are equal.

(2) The ratio of corresponding side lengths is always the same.

There are three similarities we must remember.

(1) AA Similar : Two angles of one triangle are equal to two angles of the other.

(2) SAS Similar : The ratio of two sides of a triangle is equal to that of two corresponding sides of the other, and the angles between the sides are equal to one another.

(3) SSS Similar : Each side of a triangle is a constant multiple of the corresponding side of the other triangle.

It is not enough to stress out that drawing parallel lines or perpendicular lines gives clues to find similar triangles. The following figures show the three commonly used similar triangle pairs.

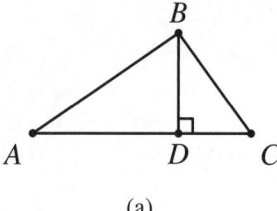 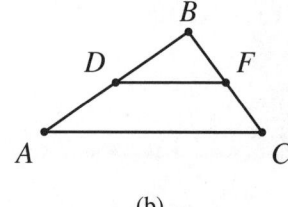 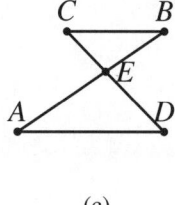
        (a)   (b)   (c)

Out of these three possible cases, part (a) comes out most because the figure contains three similar right triangles, assuming that $\triangle ABC$ is right.

- $\triangle ABC$
- $\triangle ADB$
- $\triangle BDC$

Remark

$$AB^2 = AD \cdot AC$$

$$BC^2 = CD \cdot CA$$

$$BD^2 = AD \cdot CD$$

Similar right triangles can be used to prove Pythagorean Theorem. Here is the proof of the famous theorem.

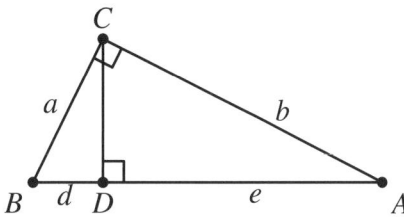

We can use $\triangle ADC \sim \triangle ACB$ to show that $b/e = c/b$, so $b^2 = ce$. Similarly, $\triangle BDC \sim \triangle BCA$ gives us $a/d = c/a$, so $a^2 = cd$. Adding these expressions for a^2 and b^2 gives us

$$a^2 + b^2 = cd + ce = c(d+e) = c^2.$$

In order to solve similar triangle problems, one should use one of the two strategies illustrated below.

(1) Draw parallel lines or perpendicular lines.

(2) Extend segments that stopped in the middle of the triangle.

Although there could be many rules to remember, these two rules are the basic steps when we attack similarity problems.

If two triangles are similar such that the sides of the larger triangle are m times the sides of the other, then the area of the larger triangle is m^2 times that of the other. Let's look at the following figure.

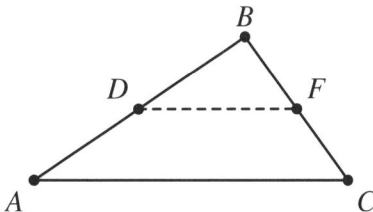

- If $\overline{DF} \parallel \overline{AC}$, then $\triangle ABC \sim \triangle DBF$.

- The length ratio $BD : BA$ turns into the area ratio of $BD^2 : BA^2$.

- If $BD = AD$ and $DF = CF$, then DF is called the *midsegment*.

Example 54

In $\triangle ABC$, X and Y are the midpoints of AB and AC, respectively. If $AB = 8, BC = 10$, and $AC = 11$, find XY.

Example 55

Given a triangle ABC where $AB = 3$, $BC = 4$, and $AC = 5$, drop the altitude from B to $\overline{AC}$ such that its perpendicular foot is D. Find BD.

Example 56

Given a triangle ABC where $AB = 13$, $BC = 14$, and $AC = 15$, let H be its orthocenter. Find BH.

Here is the solution to the examples covered in the previous page.

Example 54. Since $\overline{XY}$ is a midsegment, we get the equation $2XY = BC$. Therefore, $XY = \frac{1}{2}BC = \frac{1}{2}(10) = 5$.

Example 55. Let $BD = h$. Then, $3 \times 4 = 5 \times h$, so $h = \frac{12}{5}$.

Example 56. H produces similar triangles inside $\triangle ABC$. Hence, use similarity to figure out $BH : 5 = 5 : 4$, so $BH = \frac{25}{4}$.

HISTORICAL FACT

The mathematical study of similar triangles can be traced back to the Greek mathematicians, particularly Euclid around 300 BCE. In his foundational work, Elements, Euclid set out a systematic understanding of similarity by defining two triangles as similar if they have equal corresponding angles and proportional corresponding sides. This breakthrough provided a structured way to analyze shapes and laid the groundwork for many indirect measurement techniques, allowing for calculations without direct measurementan invaluable tool in early architecture and engineering.

One of Euclids notable contributions was establishing that similarity in triangles could serve as a gateway to understanding proportion and scale. His treatment of similar triangles as having identical shapes but different sizes also had profound implications for practical fields such as surveying and mapmaking. This allowed ancient engineers to calculate the heights of inaccessible objects, like mountains or buildings, by creating proportional relationships with smaller, similar triangles. The legacy of Euclids work on similar triangles thus extends beyond theoretical mathematics, touching various domains of human activity.

The principles of similar triangles remain a core component of geometry education, forming the basis of more advanced studies in trigonometry and calculus. In modern times, these principles continue to serve as a foundational tool, not only in fields like architecture and engineering but also in computer graphics, where understanding scale and proportional relationships is crucial for creating realistic representations. Through studying similar triangles, students not only master proportional reasoning but also cultivate analytical thinking skills essential for solving real-world problems, from scale modeling to precision engineering. Euclids work has left an enduring legacy, illustrating the profound connection between abstract mathematical ideas and practical applications.

Moreover, similar triangles offer a lens through which students explore the consistent laws of geometry that underlie both nature and human-made structures. From the symmetry in biological forms to the carefully scaled models in scientific experimentation, similarity principles allow for a simplified understanding of complex systems. This universality makes the study of similar triangles not only a key topic in mathematics but also a bridge to interdisciplinary thinking, showing how geometric concepts can provide insights into diverse fields and foster a holistic approach to problem-solving.

Walk-Through Practices

77. Given a right triangle $\triangle ABC$ with right angle $\angle B$, if $BC = 10$ and $CD = 6$, find AC.

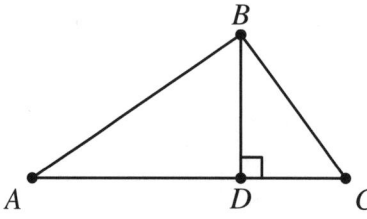

78. Points P and Q are on $\overline{AB}$ and $\overline{AC}$, respectively, such that $\overline{PQ} \parallel \overline{BC}$. Given $AB = 12$, $PB = 9$, and $AC = 18$, find QA.

79. In $\triangle ABC$, if $\angle B \cong \angle AED$ and $AD = 4$, $DB = 8$, and $AE = 6$, find CE.

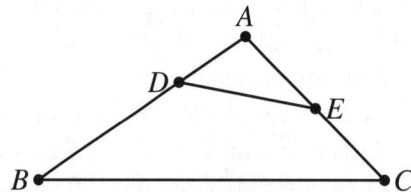

120   The Essential Guide to Geometry

80. For a given rectangle $ABCD$, if $\overline{EF}$ is a perpendicular bisector of $\overline{BD}$ and M is the point of intersection between $\overline{EF}$ and $\overline{BD}$, and $AD = 8$ and $AB = 6$, then find EF.

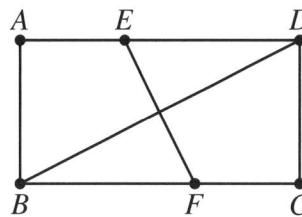

81. Given a triangle $\triangle ABC$, if G is the centroid and $\overline{AE} \parallel \overline{DF}$ and $[ABG] = 16$, then find $[CDF]$.

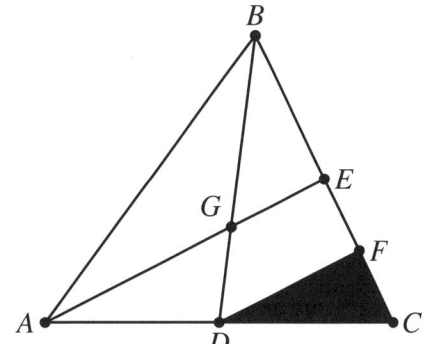

Solutions to walk-through practices can be found in the solution manual. Go to page 225.

Skill Practice

Problem 1
If a triangle *ABC* and *DEF* are similar, and they have the length ratio of 2 to 3, the area ratio must equal 4 to *n*. Determine the value of *n*.

Problem 2
According to *Triangular Inequality*, if a non-degenerate triangle *ABC* has sides of length x, 5, and 9, where x is an integer, determine the <u>number</u> of all possible values of x. (A non-degenerate triangle is a triangle with well-defined sides.)

Problem 3
According to *Triangular Inequality*, if a non-degenerate triangle *DEF* has sides of length *x*, 4, and 6, where *x* is an integer, determine the sum of all possible integer values of *x*. (A non-degenerate triangle is a triangle with well-defined sides.)

Problem 4
If a right triangle *ABC* has $AB = 10$, $BC = 24$ and $AC = 26$, let $\overline{BD}$ be the altitude from *B* to $\overline{AC}$. The length *BD* can be written as $\dfrac{m}{n}$ where *m* and *n* are relatively prime positive integers. Determine $m + n$.

Problem 5

If a right triangle DEF has $DE = 7$, $EF = 24$ and $DF = 25$, let $\overline{EG}$ be the altitude from E to $\overline{DF}$. The length EG can be written as $\dfrac{m}{n}$ where m and n are relatively prime positive integers. Determine $m + n$.

Problem 6

If a right triangle ABC has $AB = 5$, $BC = 12$ and $AC = 13$, let BD be the altitude from B to $\overline{AC}$. The length CD can be written as $\dfrac{m}{n}$ where m and n are relatively prime positive integers. Determine $m + n$.

Problem 7

If a right triangle DEF has $DE = 3$, $EF = 4$ and $DF = 5$, let EG be the altitude from E to $\overline{DF}$. The length DG can be written as $\dfrac{m}{n}$ where m and n are relatively prime positive integers. Determine $m + n$.

Problem 8

If a right isosceles triangle ABC has $AB = BC = 8$ and $AC = 8\sqrt{2}$, let $\overline{BD}$ be the altitude from B to $\overline{AC}$. The length BD can be written as $a\sqrt{b}$ where a and b are relatively prime positive integers, and b is a square-free integer. Determine $a + b$.

Problem 9
Given an obtuse triangle ABC where $AB = 8$, $BC = 6$ and $m\angle B = 120°$, the area of ABC can be written as $a\sqrt{b}$, where a and b are relatively prime positive integers, and b is a square-free integer. Determine $a + b$.

Problem 10
Given an obtuse triangle ABC where $AB = 5$, $BC = 4$ and $m\angle B = 135°$, the area of ABC can be written as $a\sqrt{b}$, where a and b are relatively prime positive integers, and b is a square-free integer. Determine $a + b$.

Answer Key

1. 9

2. 9

3. 42

4. 133

5. 193

6. 157

7. 14

8. 6

9. 15

10. 7

BEFORE YOU MOVE ON

Mass Point Geometry

Introduction: Mass Point Geometry is a powerful problem-solving technique in geometry, especially useful in solving problems involving ratios, centers of mass, and balancing conditions in triangles and other figures. The method assigns "masses" to points and uses the principles of the center of mass to simplify calculations and prove results.

Core Idea: The method is based on the concept of a weighted average. For a set of points A and B, with masses m_A and m_B, the center of mass C lies on the segment AB, and its position satisfies:

$$\frac{AC}{CB} = \frac{m_B}{m_A}.$$

Advantages:

- Provides an intuitive, physics-based approach to geometric problems.

- Reduces complex algebraic computations into straightforward balancing equations.

- Widely applicable in competitions and theoretical geometry.

Fun Fact: Mass Point Geometry leverages the physical concept of equilibrium to tackle abstract mathematical problems, making it a favorite among problem solvers.

Topic 7
Quadrilateral

7.1 Quadrilateral and Trapezoid 130

7.2 Parallelogram, Rhombus, Rectangle and Square 133

7.1 Quadrilateral and Trapezoid

A quadrilateral, such as the given figure *ABCD*, has four segments as sides, four vertices, and four angles. Nearly all quadrilaterals we consider in this section are *convex*, not *concave*. Convex quadrilaterals have all interior angles less than 180°. Concave quadrilaterals, on the other hand, have some interior angles greater than 180°.

Also, the segments connecting opposite vertices are called the diagonals of a quadrilateral. Convex quadrilaterals always have diagonals inside the figure. On the other hand, concave quadrilaterals may have diagonals outside the figure.

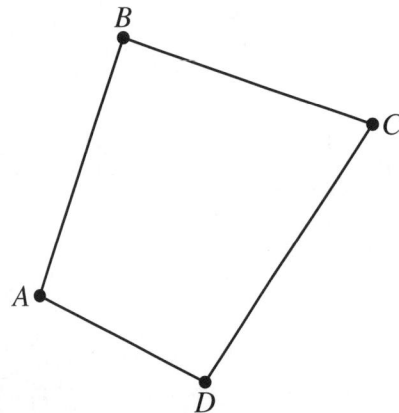

Square is both $\begin{cases} \text{Rectangle} \subset \text{Parallelogram} \subset \text{Trapezoid} \\ \text{Rhombus} \subset \text{Parallelogram} \subset \text{Trapezoid} \end{cases}$

First, we will look at a trapezoid. A trapezoid is a quadrilateral with two parallel sides. The segment connecting the midpoints of the non-parallel sides is the midsegment of the trapezoid, and the distance between the two parallel sides is the height of the trapezoid. Out of trapezoids, the most peculiar type is an isosceles trapezoid, as shown in the figure below.

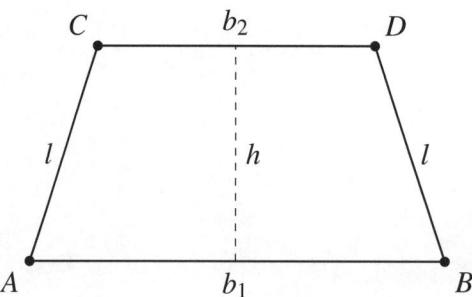

In an isosceles trapezoid:

1. The base angles are congruent.

2. The legs are congruent.

3. The diagonals are congruent.

The following examples prove that the three conditions are satisfied for a trapezoid.

130   The Essential Guide to Geometry

Example 57

If a trapezoid is isosceles, then show that each pair of base angles is congruent.

Example 58

If a trapezoid has a pair of congruent base angles, then prove that it is an isosceles trapezoid.

Example 59

Prove that a trapezoid is isosceles if and only if diagonals are congruent.

Here is the solution to the examples covered in the previous page.

Example 57. Here is the outline of the proof.
Step 1. Denote a quadrilateral ABCD such that $\overline{AB} \parallel \overline{CD}$.
Step 2. Assume the legs are congruent.
Step 3. Find E on $\overline{CD}$ such that $\overline{BE}$ is parallel to $\overline{AD}$.
Step 4. Use the proof of example 60 to deduce that $BE = AD$.
Step 5. By the assumption that $BC = AD$, conclude that $BE = BC$.
Step 6. Apply IT Theorem to deduce that $m\angle BEC = m\angle BCE$.
Step 7. Use CA Postulate to deduce that $m\angle ADC = m\angle BEC$.
Step 8. By transitivity, $m\angle ADC = m\angle BCE$.

Example 58. This is the outline of the proof.
Step 1. Denote a quadrilateral ABCD such that $\overline{AB} \parallel \overline{CD}$.
Step 2. Extend $\overline{AD}$ and $\overline{CB}$ such that they meet at E.
Step 3. $DE = CE$ by the converse of IT theorem. Step 4. CA postulate implies that $\angle EAB \cong \angle D$ and $\angle EBA \cong \angle C$.
Step 5. Thanks to transitive property, $\angle EAB \cong \angle EBA$.
Step 6. Apply the converse of IT theorem to deduce that $EA = EB$.
Step 7. Segment addition postulate shows that $AD = BC$.

Example 59. This is the outline of the proof.
Step 1. First, assume that a trapezoid is isosceles. Let it be denoted as ABCD in the same way previous examples addressed.
Step 2. Base angles are congruent by example 57.
Step 3. $\triangle ACD \cong \triangle BDC$ by ASA congruence postulate.
Step 4. CPCTC states that $AC = BD$.
Step 5. Now, assume that $AC = BD$ to prove the reverse direction.
Step 6. Let E be the point on the line $\overline{CD}$ such that $AE = AC$.
Step 7. Since $BD = AE$, use the proof of example 61 to deduce that ABDE is parallelogram.
Step 8. $m\angle AEC = m\angle ACE$ by IT Theorem.
Step 9. $m\angle AEC = m\angle BDC$ by CA postulate.
Step 10. $m\angle BDC = m\angle ACE$ by transitive property.
Step 11. $\triangle BDC \cong \triangle ACD$ by SAS congruence postulate.
Step 12. $AD = BC$ by CPCTC.

132   The Essential Guide to Geometry

7.2 Parallelogram, Rhombus, Rectangle and Square

The first triangle to investigate its properties is an isosceles triangle. Likewise, the first quadrilateral to investigate its properties is a parallelogram.

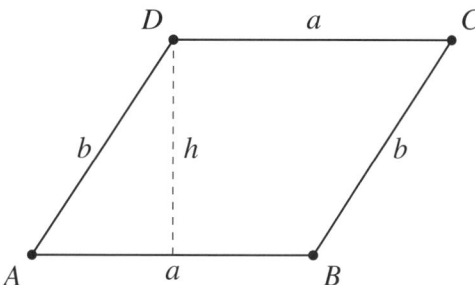

Parallelogram is a quadrilateral in which both pairs of opposite sides are parallel. Parallelogram satisfies the following four properties.

1. Opposite sides are congruent.

2. Opposite angles are congruent.

3. Two diagonals bisect each other.

4. One pair of opposite sides is congruent and parallel.

Remark

Bisected diagonals(not necessarily congruent) = Parallelogram

Example 60

Prove that the opposite sides of a parallelogram are congruent.

Example 61

If opposite sides of quadrilateral are congruent to the corresponding one, then the quadrilateral is parallelogram.

Example 62

If opposite angles of a quadrilateral are congruent to the corresponding one, then the quadrilateral is parallelogram.

Example 63

If one pair of opposite sides of a quadrilateral are both congruent and parallel, prove that it is parallelogram.

Here is the solution to the examples covered in the previous page.

Example 60. Apply ASA-congruence postulate on the two triangles formed by any diagonal, so the opposite sides must be congruent. Here is the two-column proof.

Statement	Reason
1. *ABCD* is a parallelogram with opposite sides $\overline{AB} \parallel \overline{CD}$ and $\overline{AD} \parallel \overline{BC}$.	1. Given
2. Draw diagonal $\overline{AC}$ to form $\triangle ABC$ and $\triangle CDA$.	2. Construction
3. $\overline{AB} \parallel \overline{CD}$ and $\overline{AD} \parallel \overline{BC}$.	3. Definition of parallelogram (opposite sides are parallel)
4. $\angle BAC \cong \angle DCA$ and $\angle CAD \cong \angle BCA$.	4. Alternate Interior Angles Theorem (since $\overline{AB} \parallel \overline{CD}$ and $\overline{AD} \parallel \overline{BC}$)
5. $\overline{AC} \cong \overline{AC}$.	5. Reflexive Property (shared side)
6. $\triangle ABC \cong \triangle CDA$ by ASA (Angle-Side-Angle) postulate.	6. ASA Postulate
7. $\overline{AB} \cong \overline{CD}$ and $\overline{AD} \cong \overline{BC}$.	7. CPCTC (Corresponding Parts of Congruent Triangles are Congruent)

Example 61. Apply SSS congruence postulate and the converse of alternate interior angle theorem. Here is the two-column proof.

Statement	Reason
1. Let quadrilateral *ABCD* have $\overline{AB} \cong \overline{CD}$ and $\overline{AD} \cong \overline{BC}$.	1. Given
2. Draw diagonal $\overline{AC}$ to form $\triangle ABC$ and $\triangle CDA$.	2. Construction
3. $\overline{AB} \cong \overline{CD}$ and $\overline{AD} \cong \overline{BC}$.	3. Given (opposite sides are congruent)
4. $\overline{AC} \cong \overline{AC}$.	4. Reflexive Property (shared side)
5. $\triangle ABC \cong \triangle CDA$ by SSS (Side-Side-Side) postulate.	5. SSS Postulate
6. $\angle BAC \cong \angle DCA$ and $\angle CAD \cong \angle BCA$.	6. CPCTC (Corresponding Parts of Congruent Triangles are Congruent)
7. Since $\angle BAC \cong \angle DCA$ and $\angle CAD \cong \angle BCA$, $\overline{AB} \parallel \overline{CD}$ and $\overline{AD} \parallel \overline{BC}$.	7. Converse of Alternate Interior Angles Theorem
8. Therefore, *ABCD* is a parallelogram (opposite sides are parallel).	8. Definition of a parallelogram

Example 62. Draw a diagonal. One pair of the angles is divided into two parts. Call it x and y, then the other adjacent angles must be y and x, respectively. Therefore, we get ASA-congruence postulate to get two congruent triangles. Here is the two-column proof.

Statement	Reason
1. Let quadrilateral $ABCD$ have $\angle A \cong \angle C$ and $\angle B \cong \angle D$.	1. Given
2. Draw diagonal $\overline{AC}$ to form $\triangle ABC$ and $\triangle CDA$.	2. Construction
3. Let $\angle A$ be divided into two angles, $m\angle BAC = x$ and $m\angle CAD = y$.	3. Angle splitting (definition)
4. Applying SIAT Theorem, $m\angle DCA = x$ and $m\angle BCA = y$.	4. SIAT Theorem (Sum of Interior Angles of Triangle Theorem)
5. $\overline{AC} \cong \overline{AC}$.	5. Reflexive Property (shared side)
6. $\triangle ABC \cong \triangle CDA$ by ASA (Angle-Side-Angle) postulate.	6. ASA Postulate
7. $\overline{AB} \cong \overline{CD}$ and $\overline{AD} \cong \overline{BC}$.	7. CPCTC
8. Since opposite sides are congruent, $ABCD$ is a parallelogram.	8. Definition of a parallelogram (opposite sides are congruent and parallel)

Example 63. Draw a diagonal. By parallel line property, there are two congruent alternate interior angles. Since sides are assumed to be congruent and the diagonal is a common side, we get SAS congruence.

Statement	Reason
1. $ABCD$ has $\overline{AB} \parallel \overline{CD}$ and $\overline{AB} \cong \overline{CD}$.	1. Given
2. Draw diagonal $\overline{AC}$ to form $\triangle ABC$ and $\triangle CDA$.	2. Construction
3. Since $\overline{AB} \parallel \overline{CD}$, $\angle BAC \cong \angle DCA$.	3. Alternate Interior Angles Theorem (parallel lines)
4. $\overline{AB} \cong \overline{CD}$	4. Given (opposite sides are congruent)
5. $\overline{AC} \cong \overline{AC}$.	5. Reflexive Property (shared side)
6. $\triangle ABC \cong \triangle CDA$.	6. SAS Postulate
7. $\angle ABC \cong \angle CDA$ and $\angle BCA \cong \angle CAD$.	7. CPCTC (Corresponding Parts of Congruent Triangles are Congruent)
8. Since $\angle ABC \cong \angle CDA$ and $\angle BCA \cong \angle CAD$, $\overline{AD} \parallel \overline{BC}$.	8. Converse of Alternate Interior Angles Theorem
9. $ABCD$ is a parallelogram (both pairs of opposite sides are parallel).	9. Definition of a parallelogram

Rhombus is a quadrilateral with all four congruent sides. The important property we must remember is that the diagonals are perpendicular bisector of one another. When does a parallelogram turn into a rhombus?

1. Two adjacent sides are congruent.

2. Two diagonals are perpendicular.

Let's prove that a parallelogram is a rhombus if and only if its diagonals are perpendicular.

Remark

Perpendicular diagonals are bisected = It is a rhombus.

Example 64

Prove that a parallelogram is a rhombus if and only if its diagonals are perpendicular.

Example 65

Prove that a parallelogram is a rhombus if and only if each diagonal bisects a pair of opposite angles.

Here is the solution to the examples covered in the previous page.

Example 64.
($\Rightarrow$) Assume a parallelogram is rhombus. Then, $AB = BC$, so $\angle BAE \cong \angle BCE$. Since $ABCD$ is a parallelogram, $\angle BAE \cong \angle DCE$. By SAS congruence, $\triangle BCE \cong \triangle DCE$. So, $\angle BEC \cong \angle DEC$. Two congruent angles form a linear pair. It must by 90°.

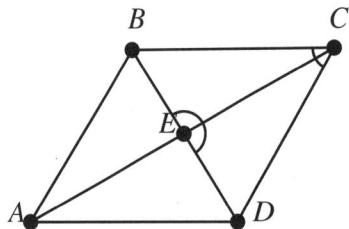

($\Leftarrow$) Assume that the diagonals of a parallelogram are perpendicular. Since diagonals are bisected, apply SAS congruence to $\triangle ABE$ and $\triangle CDE$ to get $AB = DC$. Repeat the same process to get $BC = DA$. Since BD bisect AC, we get $BC = BA$, by SAS congruence. Therefore, all four sidelengths are equal. It must be rhombus.

Example 65.
($\Rightarrow$) Assume a parallelogram is a rhombus. Then, diagonals are perpendicular bisector of one another. Therefore, we get four congruent smaller triangles, which prove that each diagonal bisects a pair of opposite angles.

($\Leftarrow$) Assume that each diagonal of parallelogram bisects a pair of opposite angles. Then, apply Pythagorean theorem to show that all sides of parallelogram are congruent. By definition, it is a rhombus.

Rectangle is a quadrilateral with all four congruent interior angles. The important property for rectangle is that the diagonals are congruent, bisecting each other. When does a parallelogram turn into a rectangle?

1. One interior angle is right angle.

2. Two diagonals are congruent.

Other than the definition of rectangle, we have to look at diagonals. Diagonals are congruent and they are bisected. This is different from isosceles trapezoid. Diagonals of isosceles trapezoid are congruent, but they are not bisected, since they are not parallelogram. However, rectangle has its diagonals congruent, bisecting each other. It is straightforward to prove that if a quadrilateral is rectangle, its diagonals are congruent, bisecting each other.

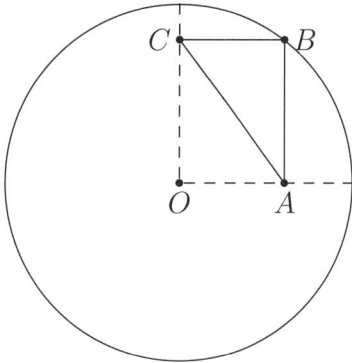

In this figure, if someone asks you to find out the length of $\overline{AC}$, where *OABC* is a rectangle, then $AC = BO$, which is the radius. Hence, without using the Pythagorean Theorem, we know that *AC* equals the radius.

Example 66

Prove that a quadrilateral is rectangle if and only if it has four right angles.

Example 67

Prove that congruent diagonals bisect each other if and only if the quadrilateral is rectangle.

Here is the solution to the examples covered in the previous page.

Example 66.
($\Rightarrow$) Assume a quadrilateral is a rectangle. Then, all four angles are congruent. By the sum of interior angles, it must be $90°$.

($\Leftarrow$) Assume that a quadrilateral has four right angles. If two lines are perpendicular to a transversal, they must be parallel. Therefore, two opposite sides are parallel. Apply same logic to the other pair of opposite sides. Therefore, this must be a rectangle.

Example 67. Assume that diagonals are congruent, bisecting each other.

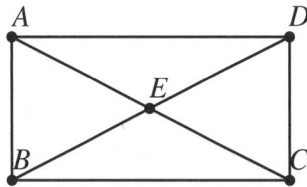

Then, by assumption, $AE = BE$, so $\angle EAB \cong \angle EBA$. Let's call its measure x. Also, $BE = CE$, so $\angle EBC \cong \angle ECB$. Let's call its measure y. Then, by the sum of interior angles of a triangle, $x+x+y+y = 180°$. Since $m\angle B = x+y$, we get $m\angle B = 90°$. Likewise, we can apply same logic to $\angle A, \angle C, \angle D$, all of which are congruent to right angle. Therefore, it is a quadrilateral.

HISTORICAL FACT

The concept of cyclic quadrilaterals—quadrilaterals that can be inscribed in a circle—has origins in ancient Greek mathematics, especially in the works of Euclid and Ptolemy. Euclid's Elements, written around 300 BCE, laid the foundations of geometry, introducing circles and the properties of quadrilaterals, which set the stage for studying cyclic figures.

Ptolemy, a Greek mathematician and astronomer of the 2nd century, expanded on these ideas with Ptolemy's Theorem. This theorem states that for a cyclic quadrilateral, the product of the lengths of its diagonals is equal to the sum of the products of its opposite sides. Ptolemy's Theorem became a critical tool in early trigonometry and astronomy, helping to solve complex problems about celestial movements and distances.

During the medieval period, Islamic scholars further explored cyclic quadrilaterals, applying them in fields such as algebra and astronomy, and contributing to the spread and evolution of geometry. Today, cyclic quadrilaterals remain a core topic in geometry, particularly in problem-solving and mathematical competitions, because of their unique properties—such as the fact that their opposite angles sum to $180°$.

The study of cyclic quadrilaterals not only enriches students' understanding of geometry but also connects them to the historical development of mathematics. By learning about these timeless concepts, students build analytical skills that are essential for tackling advanced topics in math and science.

Lastly, square is a parallelogram with four congruent sides and four right angles. Squares satisfy everything that is true about rectangles, rhombi, and parallelograms. If we let s be the side length of a square, P be the perimeter, and A the area. We have

$$P = 4s \qquad A = s^2.$$

Drawing a diagonal creates two 45-45-90 triangles. Letting the length of a diagonal be d, we have

$$d = s\sqrt{2} \qquad P = d(2\sqrt{2}) \qquad A = \frac{d^2}{2}.$$

Example 68

Prove that a quadrilateral is a square if and only it is a rhombus and rectangle.

Here is the solution to example 68.

($\Rightarrow$) Assume a quadrilateral is square. By its definition, its sides are all congruent, so it is rhombus. Its interior angles are all congruent, so it is rectangle.

($\Leftarrow$) Assume a quadrilateral is both rhombus and rectangle. Then, its sides are all congruent by the definition of rhombus. Also, its angles are all congruent by the definition of rectangle. So, it is a parallelogram whose four sides are congruent and four angles are congruent. This is simply the definition of square.

Walk-Through Practices

82. Prove that the sum of interior angles for a convex quadrilateral is 360°, whereas the sum of exterior angles for a quadrilateral is also 360°.

83. The length of median(or midsegment) of a trapezoid is equal to the average of the bases of the trapezoid.

84. Prove that two diagonals of a parallelogram bisect each other.

Statement	Reason
1. Let $ABCD$ be a parallelogram with diagonals $\overline{AC}$ and $\overline{BD}$ intersecting at point E.	1. Given
2. $\overline{AD} \parallel \overline{BC}$ and $\overline{AB} \parallel \overline{CD}$.	2. Definition of a parallelogram (opposite sides are parallel)
3. $\overline{AD} \cong \overline{BC}$.	3. Properties of Parallelogram (proved in example 60)
4. $\angle CAD \cong \angle ACB$ and $\angle ADB \cong \angle DBC$.	4.
5. $\triangle ADE \cong \triangle CBE$	5.
6. $\overline{AE} \cong \overline{CE}$ and $\overline{BE} \cong \overline{DE}$.	6. CPCTC

85. $ABCD$ is a rhombus with diagonals $AC = 8$ and $BD = 6$. Find the area and the perimeter of $ABCD$.

86. Prove that the quadrilateral formed by connecting the midpoints of a rhombus is a rectangle.

87. If ABCD and BDFG are squares, then find $[BDFG]/[ABCD]$.

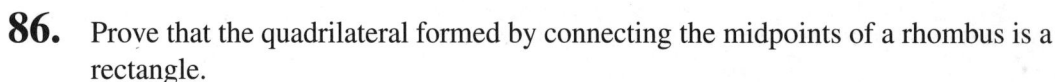

Solutions to walk-through practices can be found in the solution manual. Go to page 225.

Skill Practice

Problem 1
Given a convex quadrilateral *ABCD*, if its diagonals of length 5 and 10 are perpendicular, what is its area?

Problem 2
If two sides of a parallelogram have lengths 5 and 7, determine its perimeter.

Problem 3
Given an isosceles trapezoid *ABCD* where $\overline{AB}$ is parallel to $\overline{CD}$ such that $AB = BC = AD = 13$ and $CD = 23$, determine the value of its area.

Problem 4
If a rhombus *ABCD* has its diagonals of length 10 and 24, the perimeter must be equal to

Problem 5
A square has its side length of $3\sqrt{2}$. Find its diagonal length.

Problem 6
A rectangle has one of its diagonal with the length of 10. Find the length of the other diagonal.

Problem 7
A parallelogram $ABCD$ has the area of 112. Diagonals bisect each other at a point P. Find the area PAB.

Problem 8
A trapezoid $ABCD$ has its bases $AB = 3$ and $CD = 5$. Let diagonals be meeting at a point P. The ratio between $[ABP]$ and $[CDP]$ equals $a : b$ for relatively prime positive integers a and b. Find $a+b$.

Problem 9
A trapezoid $ABCD$ has its bases $AB = 3$ and $CD = 5$. Let diagonals be meeting at a point P. The ratio between $[ADP]$ and $[BCP]$ equals an integer value of n. Find the exact value of n.

Problem 10
Rectangle has the area of 100. Let diagonals be bisected at point P. Find the area of one of the triangles formed by this bisection.

Problem 11
There exists a convex kite whose diagonals of length 5 and 8. What is the area of this kite?

Problem 12
A parallelogram has the side lengths 6 and 8 whose interior angles are $60°$ and $120°$. The area of parallelogram can be written as $a\sqrt{b}$ where a and b are positive integers and b is a square-free integer. Compute $a+b$.

Answer Key

1. 25

2. 24

3. 216

4. 52

5. 6

6. 10

7. 28

8. 34

9. 1

10. 25

11. 20

12. 27

Topic 8
Polygons

8.1 Introduction to Polygon 150
8.2 Angle Chasing 151
8.3 Area of Polygon (Hexagon or Octagon) 153
8.4 Diagonals of Polygons 156

8.1 Introduction to Polygon

We already know what polygons are. Think about triangles and quadrilaterals. Triangles are 3-gons. Quadrilaterals are 4-gons. We can classify polygons by the following names.

Number of sides	Name
3	Triangle
4	Quadrilateral
5	Pentagon
6	Hexagon
7	Heptagon
8	Octagon
9	Nonagon
10	Decagon
11	Undecagon
12	Dodecagon

Polygon is *equilateral* if all sides are congruent. Polygon is *equiangular* if all interior angles are congruent. Polygon is *regular* if it is both equilateral and equiangular. There exists a polygon that is equilateral but not equiangular. Likewise, there exists a polygon that is equiangular but not equilateral.

Remark

Regular Polygon = Both Equilateral and Equiangular

Example 69

Name the following polygon.

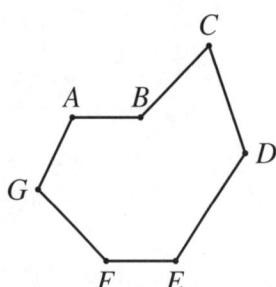

Here is the solution to example 69.
Example 69. Check that there are seven sides with seven vertices. On the other hand, the measure of one interior angle is greater than $180°$. Hence, this is a non-regular concave heptagon $ABCDEFG$.

150   The Essential Guide to Geometry

8.2 Angle Chasing

Given polygons, we are usually asked to find interior angles or exterior angles. The idea of finding the sum of interior angles comes from triangles. Cut the figure into adjacent triangles.

On the other hand, the sum of exterior angles of convex n-gon is $360°$, regardless of what n is. We did similar exercises in quadrilaterals. It is easy to show that $360°$ is not changed when $n = 3$ or $n = 4$. How can this be useful? Well, just knowing that the sum of exterior angles is $360°$ actually reduces lots of work for us. Let's go over the following examples.

Example 70

Explain why the sum of interior angles of convex n-gon is $(n-2) \times 180°$.

Example 71

Given a regular 15-gon, whose vertices are labeled from A to O, find $\angle CAB$ and $\angle COA$.

Here is the solution to the examples covered in the previous page.

Example 70. By drawing all diagonals from a fixed vertex of a polygon, we get $n-2$ diagonals. Therefore, there are $n-2$ triangles formed. Hence, the measure of the sum of interior angles is $180° \times (n-2)$.

Example 71.

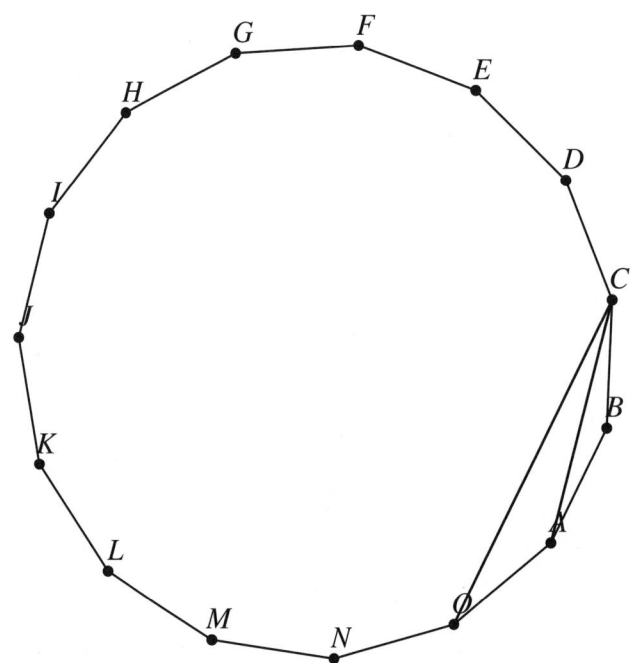

The exterior angle of B is $\dfrac{360°}{15} = 24°$. Therefore, $m\angle CAB = 12°$. Since $AC = OB$ by SAS congruent triangles and CPCTC, we get two congruent diagonals of a quadrilateral $ABCO$, which turns into an isosceles trapezoid. Therefore, $\overline{CO} \parallel \overline{AB}$. Then, $m\angle AOC = 24°$.

Remark

Regular Polygon's Interior Angle = USE EXTERIOR ANGLE

The following procedure shows how to use this remark.

1. Find one exterior angle measure.

2. Find the corresponding interior angle measure.

3. Use the property of isosceles triangle to find all relevant information.

8.3 Area of Polygon (Hexagon or Octagon)

Finding the area of polygons is the common problem style in Geometry. You may find it easy to partition areas into manageable pieces. In this section, however, we cover the properties deduced from the process of computing the area of regular polygons, which will be challenging at first glance. Let's get used to both octagon and hexagon.

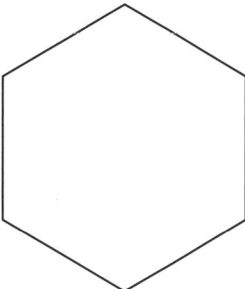

First, a regular hexagon has to do with equilateral triangle or special right triangle because it has the interior angle whose measure is equal to $120°$. This will produce $30°$ and $60°$, depending on how we cut the polygon.

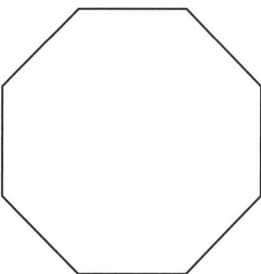

Likewise, a regular octagon deals with square or right isosceles triangle. This figure can be used to ask about length(or area) of smaller triangles formed inside the polygon.

Example 72

Compute the area of regular octagon with side length of 5.

Example 73

If *ABCDEFGH* is a regular octagon with side length of 8, find *AD*.

Example 74

Given a regular hexagon, find its area if the side length is 2.

Here is the solution to the examples covered in the previous page.
Example 72.

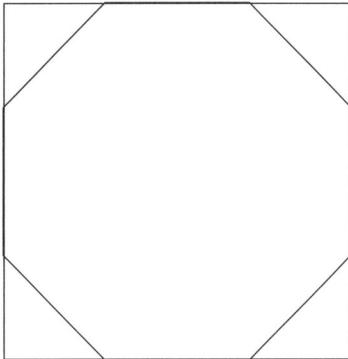

We can find the area by direct cutting, which gives two trapezoids and one rectangle. On the other hand, we can find it by using the special property of regular octagon. Octagon has its interior angle of 135°, so its exterior angle is 45°. This means we have an associated square that inscribes the octagon.

The area of a small right isosceles triangle is

$$(\frac{5}{\sqrt{2}} \times \frac{5}{\sqrt{2}})/2 = 25/4$$

Since there are four of these triangles, we get 25. The total area of a big square is

$$(5+5\sqrt{2})^2 = 25 + 50\sqrt{2} + 50 = 75 + 50\sqrt{2}$$

Subtract 25 from $75 + 50\sqrt{2}$, so we get the area of octagon $50 + 50\sqrt{2}$.

Example 73. Let $ABCDEFGH$ be our octagon. If we drop altitudes from B and C to $\overline{AD}$, we get points P and Q on $\overline{AD}$, respectively. Since $ABCD$ is a trapezoid, we get $\angle QCB = 180° - \angle CQA = 90°$, so $\angle DCQ = \angle DCB - \angle QCB = 45°$. Thus, $\triangle CDQ$ is a 45-45-90 triangle (and similarly so is $\triangle ABP$). Therefore, $AP = DQ = 4\sqrt{2}$. Since $BCQP$ is a rectangle, $QP = BC = 8$. Hence,

$$AD = AP + PQ + QD = 8 + 8\sqrt{2}$$

Example 74. Cut this hexagon into six congruent equilateral triangles. Then, *apothem*(the distance from its center to any side of a regular polygon) is equal to $\sqrt{3}$. Therefore, each equilateral triangle has the area of $\sqrt{3}$. Since there are six triangles, we get its area equal to $6\sqrt{3}$.

8.4 Diagonals of Polygons

Diagonal is formed when we connect two nonadjacent vertices. This means that there is no diagonal formed in a triangle.

Finding the number of diagonals is a common question type that appears in GPA-related exams. Here is another example of using the counts of diagonals of polygon.

Example 75

Find the total number of diagonals formed in regular pentagon.

Example 76

If a is the number of diagonals drawn from a fixed vertex of a nonagon and b is the number of triangles formed, find $a+b$.

Here is the solution to examples above.

Example 75.

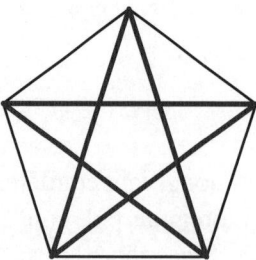

There are 5 diagonals in total.

Example 76. $a = 6$ and $b = 7$. Therefore, $a+b = 13$.

Walk-Through Practices

88. Find the number of sides in a regular polygon in which each interior angle measures $168°$.

89. If $ABCDEFGH$ is a regular octagon, find $AC : AE$.

90. Suppose that the midpoints of the sides of a regular hexagon $ABCDEF$ are joined in order to form a smaller regular hexagon $GHIJKL$, where G is the midpoint between $\overline{AB}$ and H the midpoint between $\overline{BC}$ and so on. Find the ratio of $[GBH]$ to $[ABCDEF]$.

91. Let *ABCDEF* be a regular hexagon. Find the ratio [*ACE*] : [*ABCDEF*].

92. If *ABCDEF* is a regular hexagon, find *AC* : *AD*.

93. For a concave *n*-gon, prove that the number of diagonals is equal to $\dfrac{n(n-3)}{2}$.

94. Given a regular polygon with *n* sides, if there are 11 triangles formed by drawing diagonals from a fixed vertex, what is the total number of diagonals formed by connecting any two vertices?

Solutions to walk-through practices can be found in the solution manual. Go to page 225.

Skill Practice

Problem 1
How many diagonals does a regular nonagon have?

Problem 2
How many regions are formed in a regular hexagon if all vertices are connected?

Problem 3
Given a regular hexagon $ABCDEF$, if $AB = 2$, the exact length AC can be written as $a\sqrt{b}$ where a and b are square-free positive integers. Find $a + b$.

Problem 4
Determine the sum of exterior angles of a regular decagon, in degree measures.

Problem 5
Determine the sum of interior angles of a regular heptagon, in degree measures.

Problem 6
Given a regular pentagon $ABCDE$, determine the measure of angle $\angle BAC$, in degree measures.

Problem 7
Given a regular octagon $ABCDEFGH$, if $AB = 4$, the exact length AC^2 can be written as $a + b\sqrt{c}$ where a, b, and c are positive integers such that c is a square-free integer. Determine $a + b + c$.

Problem 8
Given a regular octagon $ABCDEFGH$, the length ratio between AE and AC equals $\sqrt{x} : 1$. Find the value of x.

Problem 9
A regular dodecagon has n number of diagonals. Find the exact value of n.

Problem 10
A regular hexagon $ABCDEF$ has its area A. How many triangles of shape $\triangle ABC$ can fit A?

Answer Key

1. 27

2. 24

3. 5

4. 360

5. 900

6. 36

7. 50

8. 2

9. 54

10. 6

Topic 9
Circles

9.1 Terminology 164
9.2 Arcs, Angles and Chords 165

9.1 Terminology

Circle is the set of points equidistant from a fixed point called the center. Its distance is known as the radius. The perimeter formed by these points is called the circumference. Part of the circumference is called as arc. The following figure shows more terminology for circles.

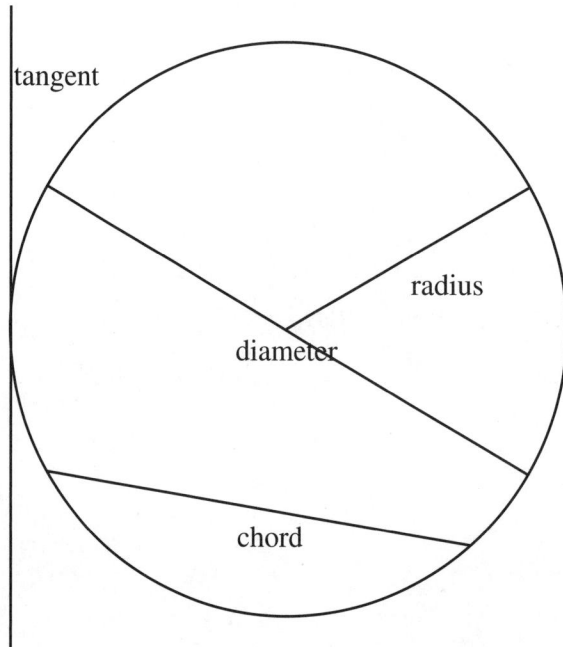

Before we move onto understanding circle properties in detail, let's write down the formula for the area and circumference of a circle.

$$A = \pi r^2$$
$$P = 2\pi r$$

Example 77

What is the radius of the circle whose area and circumference are equal in numerical values?

Here is the solution to the example above.
Example 77. Since a circle's circumference is $2\pi r$ and its area equals πr^2,

$$2\pi r = \pi r^2$$
$$2r = r^2$$
$$r = 2$$

9.2 Arcs, Angles and Chords

There is a peculiar property about circles. Length ratio, angle ratio and area ratio with respect to sectors in a given circle are all equal. Arc length and sector are proportional to the ratio of angles. We use the property of collinear points and linear pair to prove theorems on arcs and central angles. Even though we are learning about circles, we use triangles and quadrilaterals to prove theorems on circles. Oftentimes, we use SSS congruence or SAS congruence based on isosceles triangles formed by radius. Following lists of examples with figures show some basic proofs about this weird property of circle.

1. Equal arcs subtend equal central angles. (Think about cheese-cake.)

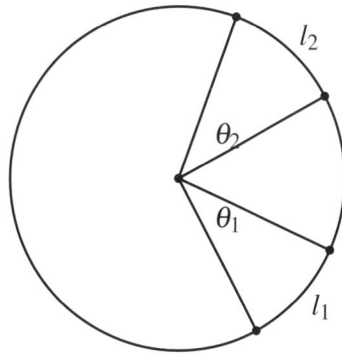

Explanation: Since $l_1 = 2\pi r \times \dfrac{\theta_1}{360°}$ and $l_2 = 2\pi r \times \dfrac{\theta_2}{360°}$, then $\theta_1 = \theta_2$.

2. If $\overline{AB}$ is a diameter of the circle O and arcCB = arcBD, then show $\angle AOC \cong \angle AOD$.

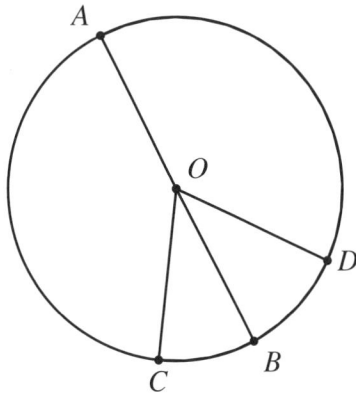

Explanation: Call $m\angle COB = x$. Then, $m\angle BOD = x$. Hence, $m\angle AOC = m\angle AOD = 180° - x$. Therefore, $\angle AOC \cong \angle AOD$.

3. Equal chords subtend equal central angles.

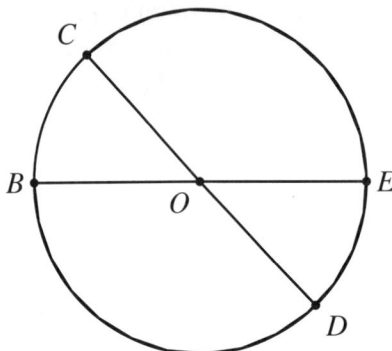

Explanation: Since $OC = OB = OE = OD$, and $BC = DE$, by assumption, we have $\triangle OBC \cong \triangle OED$ by SSS congruence. Therefore, $\angle BOC \cong \angle EOD$, by CPCTC.

Now, we will look at the relationship between the inscribed angle and the central angle and what an intercepted arc is.

4. The measure of central angle is twice that of the inscribed angle.

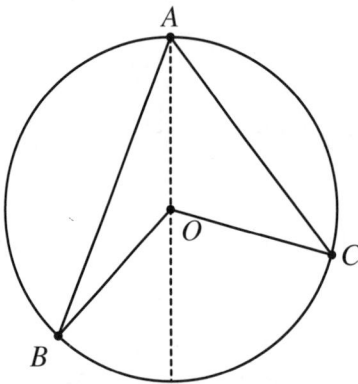

Explanation: Let $m\angle BAO = x$. Then, $m\angle ABO = x$ by isosceles triangle property. Similarly, let $m\angle CAO = y$. Then, $m\angle OCA = y$. Hence, $m\angle COB = 2x + 2y$.

The property of isosceles triangle is useful to prove theorems related to circle. Any triangle formed by the center of circle and two other points on the circle is always isosceles.

A triangle with a circle's central angle as its vertex angle is ALWAYS isosceles.

5. Show that $m\angle CAD = 2m\angle ACB$ in the figure.

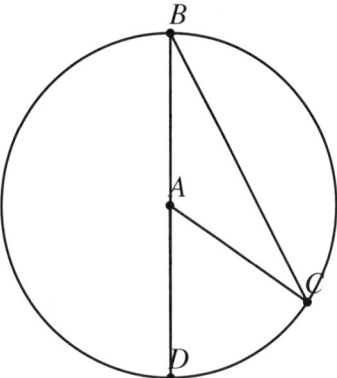

Explanation: By inscribed angle property, if we let $m\angle ABC = x$, then $m\angle CAD = 2x$. On the other hand, $\triangle ABC$ is an isosceles triangle. Therefore, $m\angle ACB = x$, so we finish the proof.

Inscribed angles of the same arc are congruent to one another.

6. Show that $\angle ABD \cong \angle ACD$ in the figure.

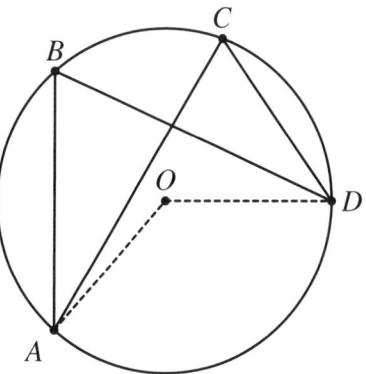

Since $2m\angle ABD = m\angle AOD$ and $2m\angle ACD = m\angle AOD$, we get $2m\angle ABD = 2m\angle ACD$. Therefore, $m\angle ABD = m\angle ACD$.

If the length of a median of a triangle is half the length of the side to which it is drawn, the triangle must be a right triangle. Moreover, the side to which this median is drawn is the hypotenuse of the right triangle.

CIRCUMDIAMETER = HYPOTENUSE

Now, let's look at the relationship between two intersecting chords. The measure of the angle formed by two intersecting chords is the average of the measures of the arcs intersected by the chords.

$$m\angle APB = m\angle CPD = \frac{\text{arc}AB + \text{arc}CD}{2}$$

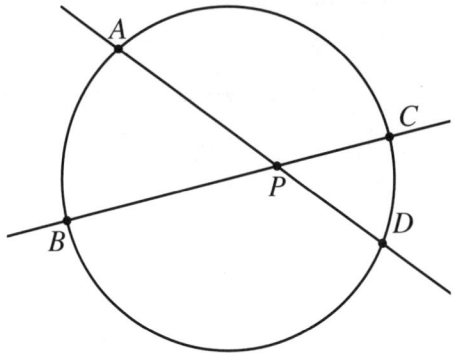

7. $m\angle APB$ is the average of the measures of arcAB and arcCD.

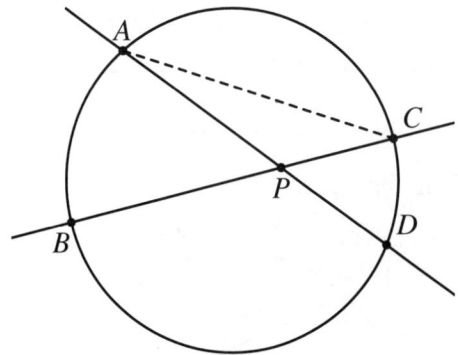

Explanation: Draw a line segment $\overline{AC}$. Then, $m\angle ACP + m\angle CAP = m\angle APB$. Since $2m\angle ACP = \text{arc}AB$ and $2m\angle CAP = \text{arc}CD$, we get

$$\frac{\text{arc}AB + \text{arc}CD}{2} = m\angle APB$$

Exactly same argument follows for $\triangle BPD$.

Similarly, two secants that meet at a point outside a circle form an angle equal to half the difference of the arcs they intercept.

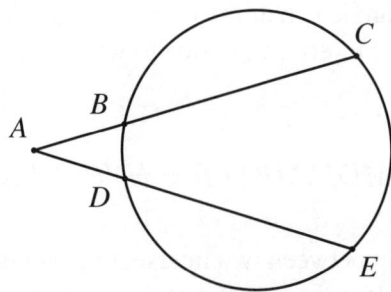

$$m\angle A = \frac{\text{arc}CE - \text{arc}BD}{2}.$$

8. $m\angle A = \dfrac{\text{arc}CE - \text{arc}BD}{2}$.

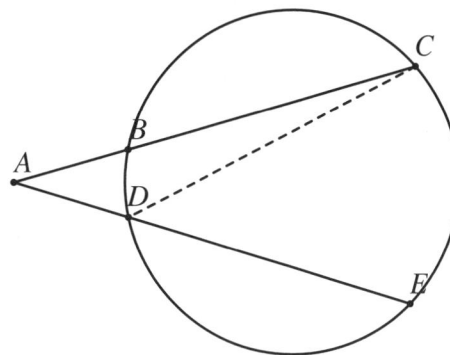

Explanation: Draw line segments $\overline{CD}$ to get $\triangle ADC$. Then, $m\angle A + m\angle ACD = m\angle CDE$. Since $2m\angle ACD = \text{arc}BD$ and $2m\angle CDE = \text{arc}CE$, some rearrangements of the terms produce

$$m\angle A = \dfrac{\text{arc}CE - \text{arc}BD}{2}$$

Exactly same argument follows for $\triangle ABE$.

Now, let's investigate about *tangents*. A tangent line is a line that touches the circle in only one point. Also, a tangent line to a circle is perpendicular to the radius drawn to the point of tangency, just as it is shown in the figure below. Conversely, a line drawn through a point on a circle that is perpendicular to the radius drawn to that point is tangent to the circle. There are *always two congruent tangents* drawn from a point outside the circle.

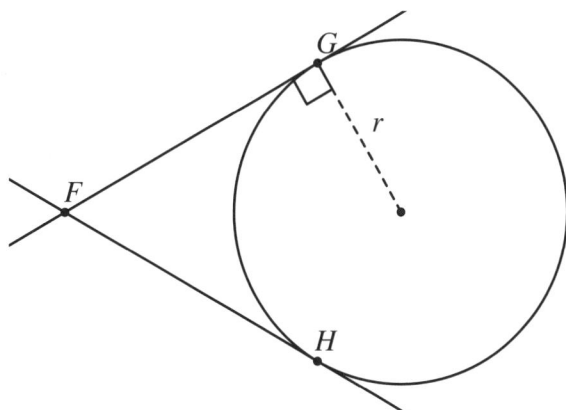

HISTORICAL FACT

The concept of tangency, central to geometry, dates back to ancient Greece. Euclids *Elements* defined tangents as lines that touch a circle at exactly one point. Apollonius of Perga further explored tangency, analyzing problems involving tangent circles and their constructions. In the Islamic Golden Age, mathematicians like Al-Tusi advanced these ideas, influencing modern geometry. Tangency later played a pivotal role in calculus, with Isaac Newton and Gottfried Wilhelm Leibniz formalizing the tangent line as a limit of secants, bridging algebra and geometry. This evolution underscores tangency's foundational role across mathematical eras.

9. If the measure of angle formed by a line and the radius is not 90°, then it is not tangent to the circle.

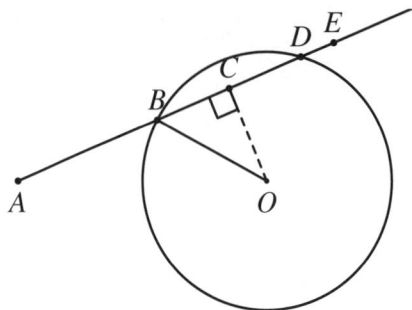

Explanation: Assume $m\angle OBE < 90°$. Then, there exists C such that $\overline{OC}$ is perpendicular to $\overrightarrow{AE}$. Since $\overline{OC}$ is the distance between a point and a line, it is the shortest distance possible. Therefore, $\overline{OB} > \overline{OC}$. Since $\overline{OB}$ is the radius of the circle, the line must cut through the circle. Consider D on the line such that $BC = DC$. Then, $\triangle BCO \cong \triangle DCO$ by SAS congruence. The line hits the circle twice, so it cannot be the tangent line, by definition. Likewise, if $m\angle OBC > 90°$, then use $\angle OBA$ instead to show that the line cuts the circle in two points.

The example above does not show that if the angle measure is 90°, the line must be tangent. Its proof, however, is easier than the previous example. Let's show this case in the following example.

10. If the measure of angle formed by the radius and the line is 90°, then the line must be tangent.

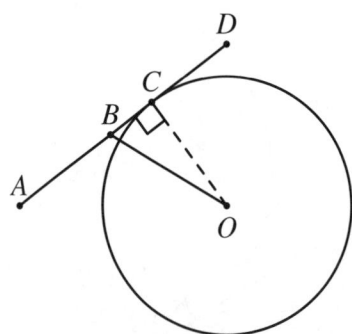

Explanation: Let B be the point on the line. Since $\triangle BCO$ is a right triangle where $\overline{BO}$ is the hypotenuse, we get $BO^2 > CO^2$, so $BO > CO$. Hence, B must stay outside the circle. Since B is an arbitrary point on the line, the line is tangent to the circle at C.

As a good application, the angle between a tangent line and a secant line can also be computed. In fact, the angle formed by a tangent and a secant is half the difference of the intercepted arcs.

Unlike triangles, not all quadrilaterals can be inscribed in a circle. Those which can be are called *cyclic quadrilaterals*. The opposite angles in a cyclic quadrilateral are supplementary. The proof is given by the following example.

11. The opposite angles in a cyclic quadrilateral are supplementary.

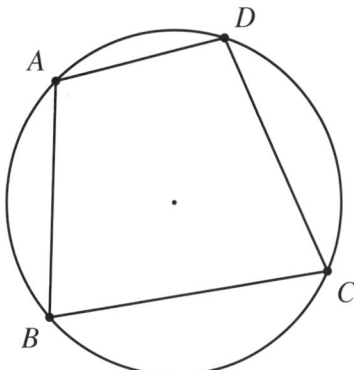

Explanation: The measures of arcs sum upto 360°. Therefore, the measures of respective inscribed angles sum upto 180°.

Now, let's delve into chord lengths equations in circle - P.o.P Theorem. The *Power of a Point Theorem* means that for all such lines, the product $(PA)(PB)$ stays unchanged, as shown in the figures below. This is called the power of point P. Applying *P.o.P Theorem* to P with respect to the circle shown gives

$$(PA)(PB) = (PC)(PD)$$

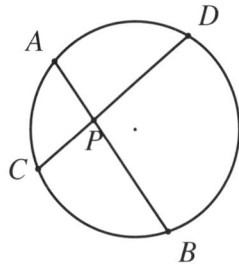

Similarly, this theorem applies for a tangent line and a secant line, as well.

$$PA^2 = (PB)(PC)$$

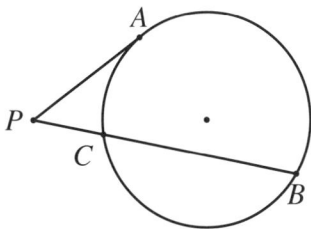

Topic_1 Basic Elements of Geometry

12. Find AB where $AP = 3$, $PC = 4$ and $PD = 6$.

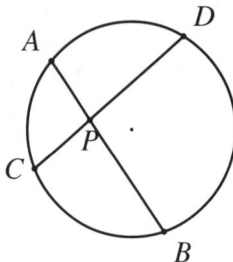

Explanation: Apply *P.o.P Theorem*. Then, $3x = 24$. Hence, $PB = 8$. Therefore, $AB = AP + PB = 3 + 8 = 11$.

13. In cyclic quadrilateral $ABCD$, $AC = 8$, $BD = 6$, $AB = 5$, and $CD = 7$. Find $AD \cdot BC$.

If ABCD is cyclic, then $AC \cdot BD = AB \cdot CD + AD \cdot BC$.

Explanation: Apply Ptolemy's Theorem to the cyclic quadrilateral. Ptolemy's Theorem states that $AC \cdot BD = AB \cdot CD + AD \cdot BC$. Substituting the given values:

$$8 \cdot 6 = 5 \cdot 7 + AD \cdot BC$$
$$48 = 35 + AD \cdot BC.$$
$$AD \cdot BC = 13.$$

Example 78

In $\triangle ABC$ we have $AB = 8$, $AC = 9$, and $BC = 10$. Point D is on the circumscribed circle of the triangle so that $\overline{AD}$ bisects $\angle BAC$. What is the value of AD/CD?

Example 79

If the inscribed angle A has the measure of 60°, what is its central angle measure?

Example 80

A circle is centered at O, $\overline{AB}$ is a diameter and C is a point on the circle with $\angle COB = 50°$. What is the degree measure of $\angle CAB$?

Example 81

In a circle centered at O, if there exist two points A and B on the circle such that $m\angle AOB = 45°$ and $OA = 4$, find the arc length of AB.

Example 82

A rectangle is circumscribed about a circle whose radius is 5. If its length and width are integers, what is the area of rectangle?

Here are the solutions to the problems above.

Example 78. Since the inscribed angles are equal, we set $BD = CD$. Let $BD = CD = k$. Then, Ptolemy's theorem states that $8k + 9k = 10AD$. Hence, $AD = \dfrac{17k}{10}$. Thus, the ratio we want equals $\dfrac{17}{10}$.

Example 79. Since the ratio between the inscribed angle and the central angle is $1 : 2$, the measure of the central angle is $120°$.

Example 80. Since $m\angle CAB$ is the inscribed angle, and its central angle is $\angle COB$, it is easy to check that $m\angle CAB = 25°$.

Example 81. Since arc ratio is equivalent to angular ratio, the arc length of AB equals $8\pi \times \dfrac{45°}{360°} = \pi$.

Example 82. The diameter is 10. Let x and y be the length and width of a rectangle. Then, $x^2 + y^2 = 100$. Hence, $(x, y) = (8, 6)$ or $(6, 8)$. The area must be 48, regardless of a pair we have.

HISTORICAL FACT

Ptolemy's Theorem, named after the ancient Greek mathematician Claudius Ptolemy, states that in a cyclic quadrilateral, the sum of the products of its two pairs of opposite sides equals the product of its diagonals. Symbolically, if $ABCD$ is cyclic, then $AC \cdot BD = AB \cdot CD + AD \cdot BC$. This theorem elegantly connects geometry and trigonometry, and is a foundational result in the study of circles.

Alexandria, a hub of ancient Greek scholarship, produced prominent mathematicians whose work shaped modern mathematics. Euclid, often called the "Father of Geometry," compiled the influential *Elements*, a cornerstone of geometric study. Heron of Alexandria, known for Heron's Formula, provided an efficient method to calculate the area of a triangle using its side lengths, laying groundwork for further geometric advancements. Claudius Ptolemy, famed for his *Almagest*, contributed significantly to astronomy and trigonometry. Hypatia, one of the first known female mathematicians, advanced Neoplatonism and wrote on geometry and algebra. These scholars exemplify Alexandria's role as a beacon of intellectual progress in the ancient world.

Brahmagupta, a 7th-century Indian mathematician, extended the study of cyclic quadrilaterals with his famous formula for their area. Known as Brahmagupta's Formula, it states that the area of a cyclic quadrilateral with sides a, b, c, and d and semi-perimeter s is $\sqrt{(s-a)(s-b)(s-c)(s-d)}$. This formula highlights the deep connection between geometry and algebra across cultures.

Walk-Through Practices

95. If $\overline{AD}$ is a diameter of a circle O and $AB = CD$, show that $\overline{BC}$ is parallel to $\overline{AD}$.

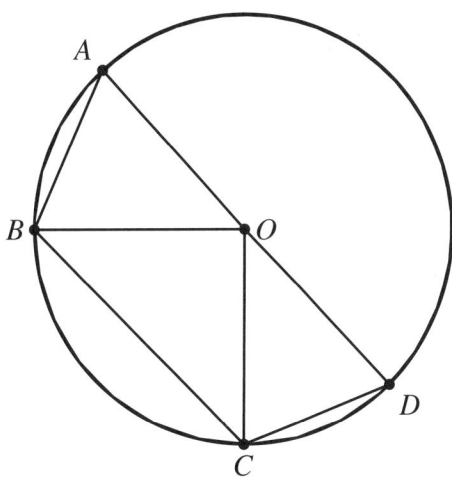

96. Find x and y in the following figure.

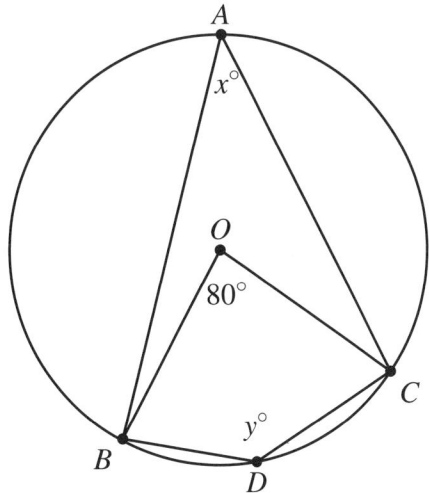

Topic_1 Basic Elements of Geometry

97. If $BC = 3$, $CE = 5$, and $CD = 4$, find AC.

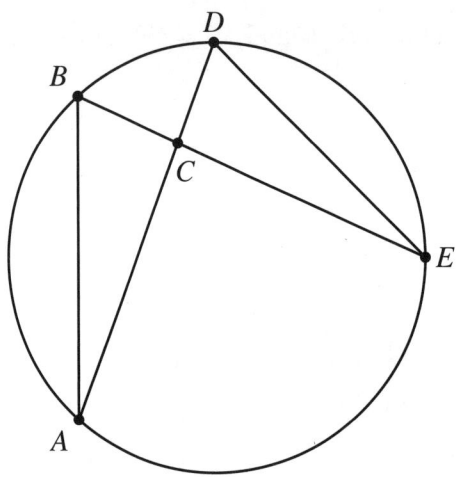

98. Find CD if $BC = 2$ and $BO = 2$.

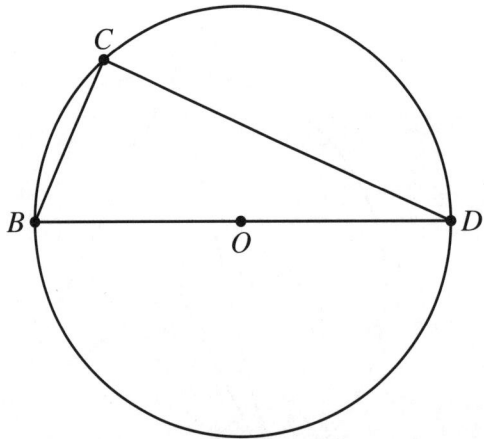

99. Assume a line *l* is tangent to a circle at point *T*. If point *A* is on the circle such that arc$AT = 70°$, find the acute angle formed by chord $\overline{AT}$ and line *l*.

100. In the following diagram, arc$IH = 150°$ and arc$IJ = 80°$. If $\overline{IG}$ is tangent to the circle at B, where G, J, and H are collinear, find m$\angle IGH$.

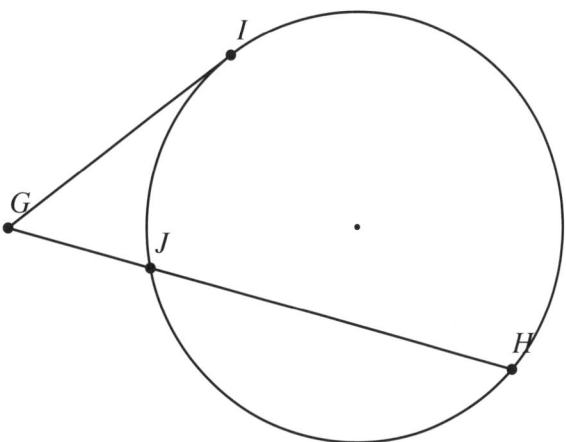

101. Given an isosceles triangle $\triangle ABC$ such that $AB = AC$, if P is the point of intersection between the chord AD and BC, show that $AB^2 = (AP)(AD)$.

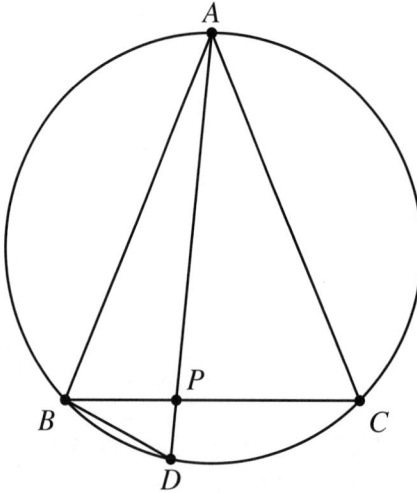

Solutions to walk-through practices can be found in the solution manual. Go to page 225.

Skill Practice

Problem 1
Given a circle of radius 10, determine the length of the longest chord.

Problem 2
A circle of radius 3 has the circumference $k\pi$ where k is an integer. Determine the exact value of k.

Problem 3
A circle of radius 17 has the area of $n\pi$ where n is an integer. Determine the exact value of n.

Problem 4
If the inscribed angle has the measure of $45°$, what is the measure of its central angle?

Problem 5
If an arc AB has the measure of $40°$, find the measure of its arbitrary inscribed angle, in degrees.

Problem 6
If an arc BC has the measure of $60°$, find the measure of its central angle, in degrees.

Problem 7
If two chords $\overline{AB}$ and $\overline{CD}$ meet at a point P inside the circle, where $AP = 2$, $BP = 6$, $CD = 7$ such that PC and PD are positive integers where $PC < PD$, find PD.

Problem 8
If the extended lines containing two different chords $\overline{AB}$ and $\overline{CD}$ meet at a point P outside the circle, where $AB = 4$ and $AP = 2$, find the integer value of CD if $CP = 1$. (Note that $DP > CP$.)

Problem 9
Two externally tangent circles have radii 9 and 1. Determine the length of one of the external tangents.

Problem 10
Two circles with radii 2 and 8 are apart by 12 units. The length of one of the external tangents can be written as $\sqrt{n}$ where n is a positive integer. Determine the value of n.

Answer Key

1. 20

2. 6

3. 289

4. 90

5. 20

6. 60

7. 4

8. 11

9. 6

10. 108

BEFORE YOU MOVE ON

Brahmagupta's Formula

Statement of the Formula: Brahmagupta's Formula provides a method to calculate the area of a cyclic quadrilateral (a quadrilateral that can be inscribed in a circle) using its side lengths. If a cyclic quadrilateral has sides a, b, c, and d, and its semi-perimeter is:

$$s = \frac{a+b+c+d}{2},$$

then the area K of the quadrilateral is given by:

$$K = \sqrt{(s-a)(s-b)(s-c)(s-d)}.$$

This formula generalizes Heron's formula for triangles, as a triangle can be seen as a cyclic quadrilateral with one side of length zero.

Conditions for Application:

- The quadrilateral must be cyclic (opposite angles sum to $180°$).

- The side lengths must be known to compute the semi-perimeter.

Historical Note: Brahmagupta (598668 CE) was a brilliant Indian mathematician and astronomer. His contributions, including Brahmagupta's Formula, laid the foundation for advancements in algebra and geometry.

Topic 10

Transformation

10.1 Translation and Rotation..184
10.2 Reflection and Dilation...187

10.1 Translation and Rotation

We can describe a translation using coordinates. Sliding a figure to the right or left corresponds to increasing or decreasing its *x*-coordinate. Similarly, moving up or down is increasing or decreasing the *y*-coordinate. Thus, to translate a figure *a* units to the right and *b* units up, we would apply the mapping $x' = x + a$ and $y' = y + b$, where (x', y') are the coordinates of the new figure, the image. We could also write this as $(x', y') = (x + a, y + b)$ or $(x, y) \to (x + a, y + b)$; in Cartesian coordinates, all are equivalent to the desired translation.

Another way to remember translation is a vector notation. We are simply pushing the point to vertical or horizontal distance of fixed units. This is, in fact, a good example of introducing vectors.

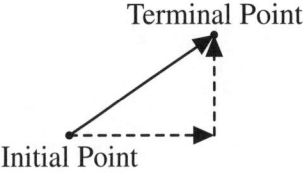

A vector is a quantity that has both magnitude and direction. We usually denote this by $[a, b]$ meaning that we push a point *a* units right and *b* units up. Naturally, we get associated parallelograms when we translate the given object, as we can check from the following figure.

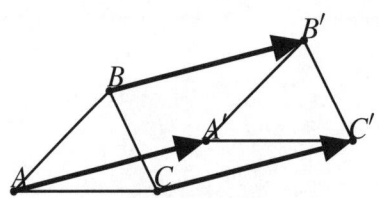

Notice that the translation(or slide) of each point has same distance. In our example, AA', BB' and CC' all have the same distance. This is not true for reflection.

In a rotation, one point, the center of rotation, is fixed and everything else rotates about it. Since we can turn in two directions, we generally have to specify a direction, clockwise or counterclockwise, as well as an angle.

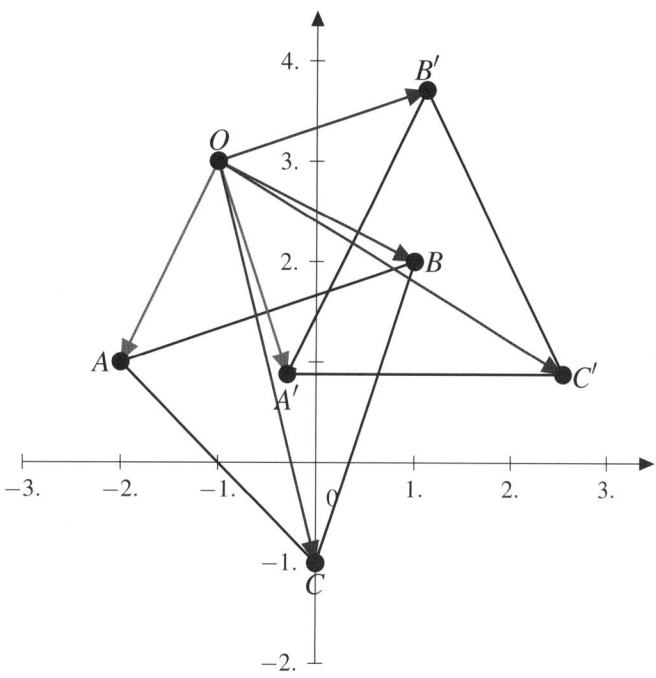

The distance of any point from the center of rotation is the same as the distance from the image of the point to the center. The figure above satisfies

$$m\angle AOA' = m\angle BOB' = m\angle COC' = 45°$$

and

$$OA = OA', OB = OB', OC = OC'$$

In doing any rotation, make sure you are rotating in the proper direction if a direction is specified.

Like translations, rotations map figures to congruent figures; however, unlike translations, a rotation changes the orientation of the figure in the plane. In particular, we know that $AB = A'B'$ and $OA = OA'$. Many rotation problems are solved by using these distance preserving qualities of rotation and the definition of angle of rotation (the angle formed by connecting the center to any point and its image).

Remark

Rotation about the center = Isosceles Triangles

Example 83

A fixed point of a transformation is a point whose image is the same as itself. Does any translation have fixed points?

Example 84

Let O be the center of equilateral $\triangle XYZ$.
(a) Through what angle(s) between $0°$ and $360°$ can we rotate Y about Z such that the result is point X?
(b) Through what angle(s) between $0°$ and $360°$ can we rotate X about O such that the result is point Y?
(c) Is there a rotation about Y that maps O to Z?

Here are the solutions to the examples covered above.

Example 83. Every point(or every figure) in the plane moves the same distance under a translation. If there is a fixed point, that point moves distance 0, so all points move the distance of 0. Thus the only translation which has a fixed point is the trivial translation $(x',y') = (x,y)$.

Example 84. (a) Since $YZ = XZ$ and $\angle YZX = 60°$, a $60°$ rotation clockwise about Z takes Y to X. Of course, a $300°$ rotation the other way will also do the job!

(b) Since O is the center of equilateral $\triangle XYZ$, $\overline{XO}$ and $\overline{YO}$ bisect $\angle ZXY$ and $\angle ZYX$, respectively. Therefore, $\angle YXO = \angle OYX = 30°$, so

$$\angle XOY = 180° - \angle YXO - \angle OYX = 120°.$$

Since $OX = OY$ and $\angle XOY = 120°$, if we rotate X $120°$ counterclockwise about O, it is mapped to point Y. Note that we can also rotate X $240°$ clockwise around O to get to Y.

(c) By the definition of rotation, every rotation about Y maps O to a point that is as far from Y as O is. Since $\overline{YO}$ and $\overline{YZ}$ are not equal in length (make sure you see why!), it is impossible for a rotation about Y to map O to Z.

10.2 Reflection and Dilation

There are two types of reflection. There are reflections about the line and about the point. Let's look at the reflection about the line.

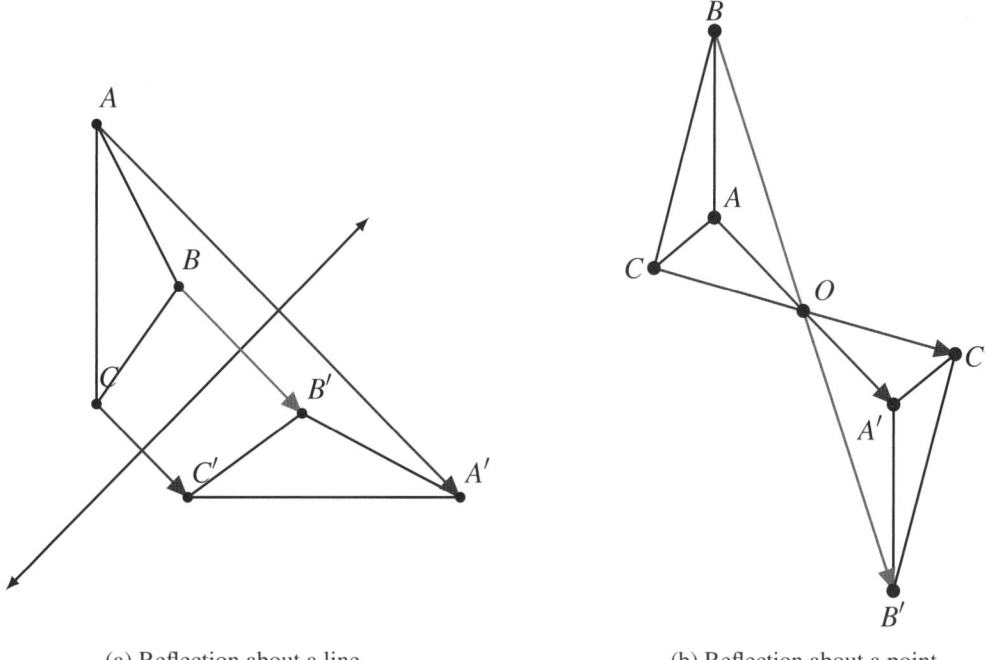

(a) Reflection about a line   (b) Reflection about a point

A line of reflection is like a mirror. When we reflect a figure in a line, we map every point on that figure to a point which is symmetric to the original point with respect to the line. Thus, any point and its image are the same distance from the line in which the point is reflected, and this line is perpendicular to the segment connecting a point and its image.

The difference between the previous two transformations and reflection is that the reflection does not preserve vector length. From our figures, the lengths of red vectors, blue vectors, and purple vectors are different from one another. However, the midpoints of the original point and the image of the transformation are all collinear, given that there is a line of symmetry.

The point of reflection, unlike the line of symmetry, is the point of concurrency of all midpoints of the original points and the images of the transformation, as one can check from the following figure.

Remark
Reflection along a line or a point = Midpoint

Dilation is either a stretch or shrink. Let's look at the following figure to understand this transformation.

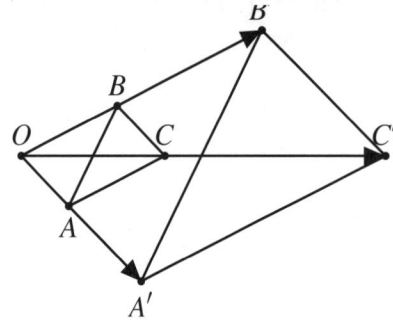

Point O is the center of dilation, where the scale factor is 2.5, so $OA'/OA = 2.5$. In fact, the image of P upon dilation with scale factor of k and the center of dilation O is $OP' = k(OP)$ where k is positive. By the way, the scale factor does not have to be positive. The following diagram has the scale factor of -1.5 such that $OA' : OA = 3 : 2$.

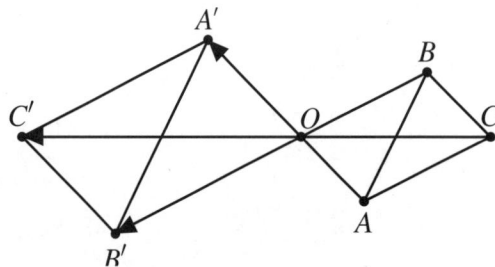

Example 85

How many lines of symmetry does the following figure have?
(a) Rectangle(not a square)
(b) Parallelogram(not rectangle nor rhombus)
(c) A regular n-gon?

Example 86

Given the center of dilation $(0,0)$, find the image after the dilation of $\triangle ABC$ where $A = (1,2), B = (3,1), C = (2,5)$ by a scale factor of 2.

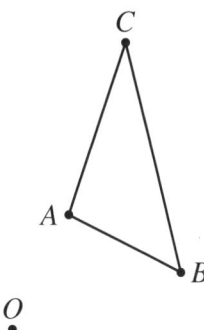

Here are the solutions to the examples covered above.

Example 85. (a) There are 2 lines of symmetry passing through the midpoints of opposite sides.

(b) There is no line of symmetry.

(c) There are n lines of symmetry. If n is even, then a line connecting a vertex to the opposite vertex is the line of symmetry. If n is odd, a line connecting a vertex to the midpoint of the opposite sides is the line of symmetry.

Example 86. By a scale factor of 2, $OA'/OA = OB'/OB = OC'/OC = 2$. Hence, $A' = (2,4), B = (6,2), C = (4,10)$.

Walk-Through Practices

102. If $A = (-2, 1), B = (1, 2), C = (0, -1)$, find the coordinates of A', B', C' if the transformation is given by $(x', y') = (x + 1, y - 2)$.

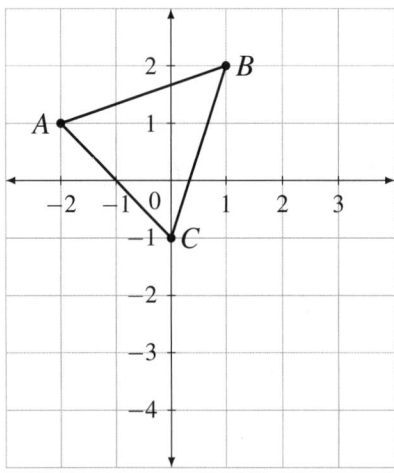

103. Suppose $ABCDEFGH$ is a regular octagon, and we perform a translation. If it sends A to F, find the image after sending B by this translation.

104. Given a figure, suppose 35° rotation about some point *P* coincides exactly with the original figure. Determine whether a rotation about 25° about *P* coincides with the figure.

105. Given a equilateral triangle *ABC*, if it is rotated about 60° clockwise about the centroid *G*, determine the polygon formed by connecting the vertices of the rotated figure and those of the original figure.

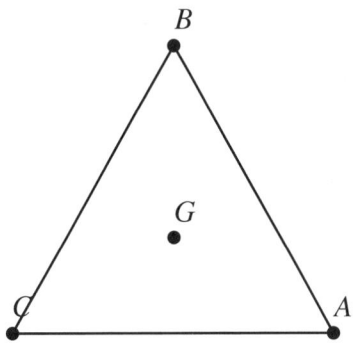

106. Square $ABCD$ is reflected over $\overleftrightarrow{AB}$. C' and D' are the images of C and D, respectively. Given $AB = 3$, find $C'D$.

107. Rachel has a house 5 miles north of a parking lot that goes east-west. She has to go to her office, 2 miles north of the parking lot, and 4 miles west and 3 miles south of her house. She must reach the parking lot to go to her office, then walk to the house. What is the shortest path?

108. Shrink △ABC about O by a scale factor of 2.

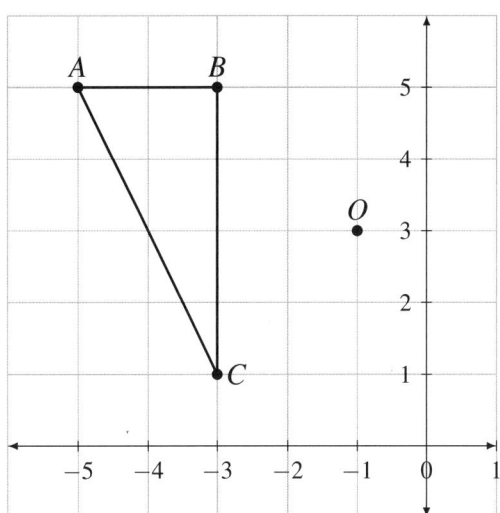

Skill Practice

Problem 1
Given a vector $v = <4, 1>$, its direction implies that we shift x unit right and y units up. Determine the sum $x + y$.

Problem 2
Given a vector v and u, if $v = <2, 4>$ and $u = <1, 5>$, if $u + v = <a, b>$ for some a and b, determine the sum $a + b$.

Problem 3
Given a triangle ABC where $AB = 5$, $BC = 12$, and $AC = 13$, if translation vector $(x', y') = (x + 3, y + 4)$ is imposed upon the triangle, what should be the area of the resulting triangle $A'B'C'$?

Problem 4
If $(5, -2)$ is rotated $90°$ counterclockwise about $(0, 0)$, the resulting point must be written as (a, b). Determine the sum $a + b$.

Problem 5
Given a scale factor of 3, if a triangle ABC is stretched from O with the scale factor into $A'B'C'$, the area ratio of $A'B'C'$ to ABC can be written as an integer value of n. Determine the exact value of n.

Problem 6
If $(-5,2)$ is rotated $180°$ counterclockwise about $(0,0)$, the resulting point must be written as (a,b). Determine the sum $a+b$.

Problem 7
If $(-3,4)$ is rotated $180°$ counterclockwise about $(0,0)$. The image is exactly equal to the reflection of $(-3,4)$ about the point (a,b). Find $a+b$.

Problem 8
A point $A(3,2)$ is scaled by a factor of 2 from the center of dilation $(0,0)$. The image of the scale can be plotted as (a,b). Find $a+b$.

Problem 9
Point $(5,4)$ is reflected about the line $y=x$. The image is located at (a,b). Find $a+b$.

Problem 10
A point $(6,6)$ is reflected about the line $y=0$ to reach $(0,2)$. Find the length of shortest path via this reflection.

Answer Key

1. 5

2. 12

3. 30

4. 7

5. 9

6. 3

7. 0

8. 10

9. 9

10. 10

Topic 11
Solid Figures

11.1 Polyhedron and Solids of Revolution 198
11.2 Surface Area 202
11.3 Volume 206

11.1 Polyhedron and Solids of Revolution

Solid figures we study in Geometry are either polyhedron or not. A polyhedron is a solid figure whose faces are planar polygons. There are no curved surfaces in polyhedron. In other words, spheres, cylinders, and cones are not considered polyhedron. Here are some vocabularies we should know before we move on.

- Face : Polygon(s) on the surface of the solid.

- Edge : Side intersection of adjacent faces

- Vertices : Point intersection of edges.

We usually study two types of solids we will focus on : prisms and pyramids. What are they? Prisms are solid figures in which the bases are two parallel and congruent faces, and the lateral faces are parallelograms formed by connecting corresponding vertices of the bases. On the other hand, pyramids are solid figures with one polygonal face and all other faces triangles with a common vertex is called a pyramid.

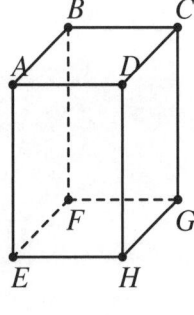 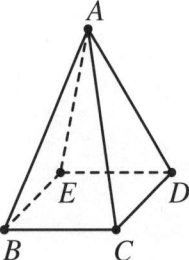

(a) Prisms   (b) Pyramids

A polyhedron is a solid figure whose faces are planar polygons. There are no curved surfaces in a polyhedron. Cubes, parallelepipeds, prisms, and pyramids are all examples of polyhedrons. A regular polyhedron is a polyhedron whose faces are all congruent regular polygons and whose vertices are met by the same number of faces. The table provides information about the only five regular polyhedra, which are the only possible polyhedra. Since regular polyhedra are three dimensional figures, a vertex has three faces converging at it. Also, the sum of angles should be less than 360° to produce a three dimensional figure. Therefore, the only possible faces for regular polyhedra are equilateral triangles, squares and regular pentagons.

Name	Shape of Faces	# of Faces	# of Vertices	# of Edges
Tetrahedron	triangles	4	4	6
Hexahedron	squares	6	8	12
Octahedron	triangles	8	6	12
Dodecahedron	pentagons	12	20	30
Icosahedron	triangles	20	12	30

Looking over these numbers of faces, vertices, and edges, we note that for each of these special polyhedra, the number of edges is 2 less than the sum of the number of faces and the number of vertices. This is no accident. In fact, for any polyhedron, regular or not, it is true that

$$(\# \text{ vertices}) + (\# \text{ faces}) - (\# \text{ edges}) = 2.$$

Although the five polyhedra shown above are the only regular polyhedra, they are certainly not the only polyhedra whose faces are regular polygons. Look at a soccer ball; the hexagons and pentagons which make up the surface are all regular polygons. These five polyhedra are great resources for teachers to make a multiple choice question, as the concept can be easily applied to produce examples like the following one.

On the other hand, a solid of revolution is a solid figure produced by rotating a planar figure about the axis of rotation. We either have sphere, cylinder, or cone, where hemisphere is not a solid of revolution. A sphere is just a ball. Just as a circle is the set of all points in a plane which are a fixed distance from a given point, a sphere is the set of all points in space which are a fixed distance from a given point. As with the circle, the fixed point is the center, and the distance is the radius of the sphere.

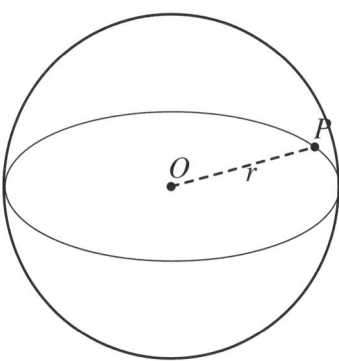

If a plane intersects a sphere, the intersection is either a point (if the plane is tangent to the sphere) or a circle. The intersection of a sphere and a plane passing through its center is called a great circle of the sphere.

GEOMETRICAL INSIGHT

The formula for a sphere's surface area, $4\pi r^2$, derives from integrating circles along a spheres radius. Imagine a baseball: its stitching mimics four great circles, highlighting the sphere's symmetry. It is easy to remember the surface area formula this way.

Likewise, the volume of a sphere, $\frac{4}{3}\pi r^3$, comes from stacking infinitesimal disks along its radius. Picture slicing a watermelon: as you carve through, the curved slices build its 3D shape. This will help you understand the formula better.

Example 87

Which of the following regular polyhedron whose faces are triangles that has 30 edges in total?
(A) Tetrahedron
(B) Hexahedron
(C) Octahedron
(D) Dodecahedron
(E) Icosahedron

Example 88

What solid figure would be produced if the plane figure is rotated about l once?

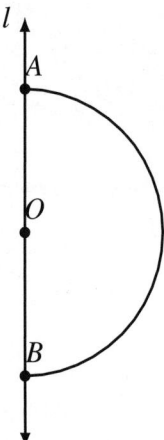

Here are the solutions to the examples covered above.

Example 87. The answer is (E). As we can check from the table above, it must be icosahedron(a regular 20-hedron).

Example 88. It is a sphere centered about O whose radius is OA.

The next example is a cone. A circular cone has a circle as a base, and a right circular cone is a regular pyramid with a circular base. Thus the foot of the altitude of a right circular cone is the center of the circular base. If we let r be the radius and h the altitude, the volume is $\pi r^2 h/3$. The lateral surface area is the area of the curved surface. We define the slant height, l, of a right circular cone as the distance from the vertex, which is sometimes called the apex, to the boundary of the circular base.

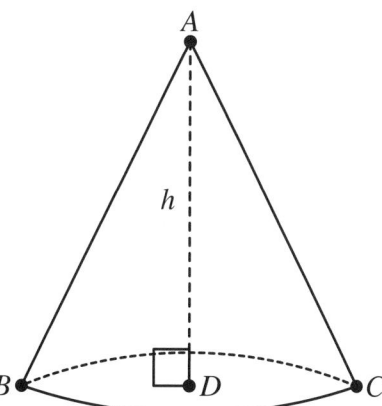

Last example is a cylinder. A cylinder is a prism whose bases are curved surfaces rather than polygons. A circular cylinder has bases which are circles, and a right circular cylinder is a right prism whose bases are circles. A typical can is a right circular cylinder. The line joining the centers of the bases is called the axis of the cylinder.

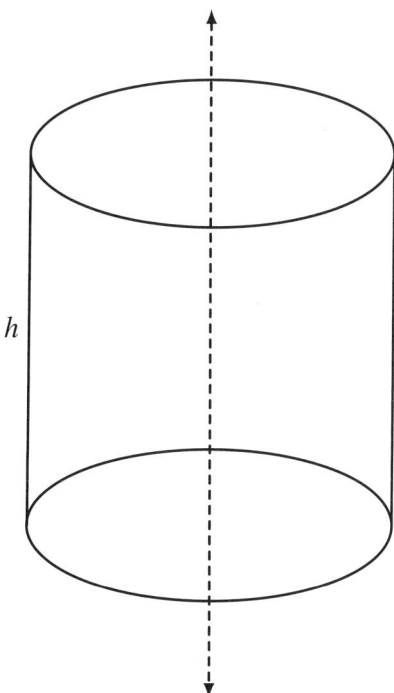

11.2 Surface Area

Surface area of polyhedron is the sum of the areas of all faces. There are base areas and lateral areas. Lateral area is the sum of the areas of lateral faces.

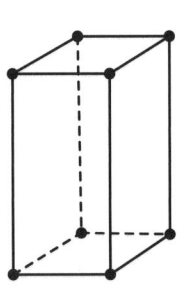
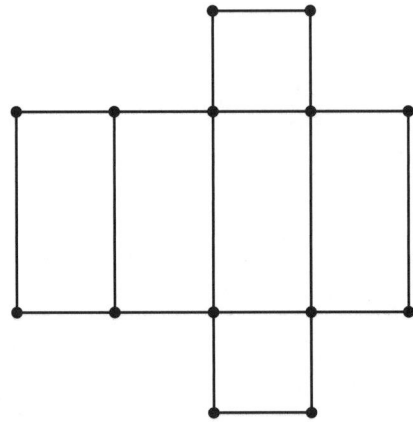

As we can see from the figure above, net is a planar representation of the faces. When we compute the net area, we divide it into two parts : lateral area and base area. Questions for computing surface area are straightforward. The following formula tells us the surface area of solids.

- Prism : Base Perimeter $\times$ height $+ 2\times$ Base Area
- Cube : $6\times$ Base Area
- Pyramid : $1/2\times$ Base Perimeter $\times$ Slant height $+$ Base Area
- Cylinder : $2\pi r \times$ height $+ 2 \times \pi r^2$
- Cone : $\pi r l + \pi r^2$
- Sphere : $4\pi r^2$.

Also, recall that the ratio of circle depends on the ratio of central angles.

$$\frac{\text{Central Angle}}{360°} = \frac{\text{Arc Measure}}{\text{Circumference}} = \frac{\text{Area of Sector}}{\text{Area of Circle}}$$

Remark

Area units are ALWAYS in **square units**.

Volume units are ALWAYS in **cubic units**.

Example 89

Suppose we cut the following solid of revolution by a plane that contains the axis of rotation. Find the area of the planar figure.

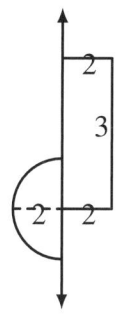

Example 90

What is the surface area of a cylinder that fits inside a cube of side length of 4 units?

Example 91

Find the surface area of the following right pyramid. Assume that the base is a square.

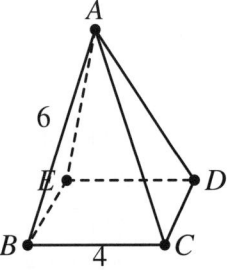

Example 92

Derive the formula of the lateral surface area of a cone.

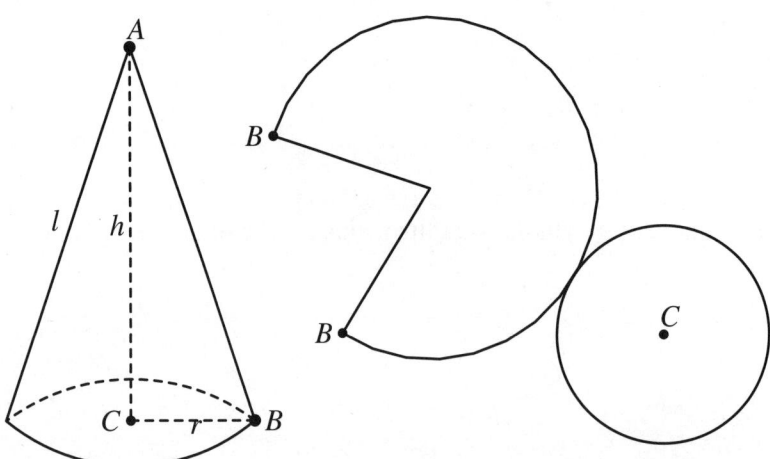

Here are the solutions to the examples in the previous page.

Example 89. We get $4 \times 3 = 12$ for rectangle and 2π for semicircle. Therefore, $12 + 2\pi$ is the area.

Example 90. The radius of the base must be 2 units, so the area of two bases must be $2 \times 4\pi$ square units. On the other hand, the lateral area must be $4 \times 4\pi$ square units, so the surface area must be 24π square units.

Example 91. First, we need to get the slant height. Slant height is given by Pythagorean Theorem so that it becomes $4\sqrt{2}$. Hence, by the formula we get $32\sqrt{2} + 16$.

Example 92. Sector Area : Circle Area = Arc Length : Circumference. Hence, Sector Area : $\pi l^2 = 2\pi r : 2\pi l$. Therefore, the area of sector is $\pi r l$.

HISTORICAL FACT

A regular polyhedron, also known as a Platonic solid, is a convex polyhedron with congruent faces of regular polygons and identical vertices. There are exactly five regular polyhedra: the tetrahedron, cube, octahedron, dodecahedron, and icosahedron. These solids have fascinated mathematicians, artists, and scientists for millennia due to their symmetry and aesthetic appeal.

The study of regular polyhedra dates back to ancient Greece, where the philosopher Plato associated each solid with an element in his cosmology: fire (tetrahedron), earth (cube), air (octahedron), water (icosahedron), and the heavens (dodecahedron). Euclid systematically described these solids in the "Elements," providing a rigorous mathematical foundation. Archimedes extended this work by exploring semi-regular solids, which also exhibit symmetry but allow for more variation in face types.

Across cultures, regular polyhedra have symbolized harmony and order. In Renaissance Europe, Johannes Kepler studied their connections to planetary orbits, inspiring his model of the solar system. Leonardo da Vinci, an artist and scientist, illustrated these shapes beautifully in Luca Pacioli's *De Divina Proportione*, emphasizing their role in art and nature.

In the cult classic sci-fi film "The Fifth Element," Platonic solids take on a cosmic and symbolic role. The dodecahedron, associated with the heavens in Platonic thought, parallels the film's mystical fifth element, representing unity and harmony. The film's imaginative universe weaves mathematical symbolism with futuristic storytelling, reminding us of the enduring allure of these geometrical forms in both ancient philosophy and modern pop culture.

11.3 Volume

Let's look at prisms and cylinders, whose volumes are given by $V = Bh$. Right prisms and right cylinders are easy to compute.

- Right prism : Base area × height
- Right cylinder : $\pi r^2 \times$ height

What if the solid is oblique? Then, we use Cavalieri's principle, which is applied to the volumes of all solids. Here is the principle.

Two solids that have the same height and same cross-sectional area have the same volume.

Sphere, on the other hand, has its volume given by $\frac{4}{3}\pi r^3$. Imagine there are small copies of pyramids whose height is r and the base area is a small portion of the surface area of the sphere. Then, if we add them up, we get $\frac{1}{3} \times r \times 4\pi r^2$.

Example 93

Find the volume of the following oblique cylinder if the radius is 5.

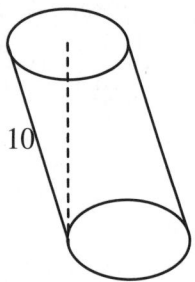

Example 94

Find the volume of a hemisphere whose diameter is 10cm.

Here are the solutions to the examples covered above.

Example 93. The height of this oblique cylinder is $5\sqrt{3}$ by a special right triangle ratio. Therefore, the base area, which is 25π, times the height, which is $5\sqrt{3}$ result in $125\sqrt{3}\pi$.

Example 94. Since the volume of a hemisphere is half the volume of the sphere, we first compute the volume of the sphere. The radius is $5cm$, so its volume must be $\frac{4}{3}\pi(5)^3 cm^3$. Here, we take half of its value, so the volume of a hemisphere is equal to $\frac{250}{3}\pi cm^3$.

HISTORICAL FACT

Cavalieri's Principle, named after the Italian mathematician Bonaventura Cavalieri, provides a powerful method to calculate volumes of solids. It states that if two solids have the same height and their cross-sectional areas are equal at every level, then their volumes are also equal.

Imagine slicing a loaf of bread and a cake of identical shape and height. If every slice of the bread has the same area as the corresponding slice of the cake, their volumes must be identical.

Cavalieri's Principle underpins many famous results, such as the volume of a sphere or a cone. By comparing the sphere to a cylinder minus a cone, Cavalieris method offers an intuitive understanding of 3D space. Its simplicity and versatility continue to inspire mathematicians and educators alike.

Walk-Through Practices

109. Find the regular polyhedron whose number of faces that converge at a vertex is 3 and whose total number of edges is 30.

110. Determine whether each statement is true. If the statement is false, explain why.

(a) The axis of cylinder is perpendicular to the base.

(b) The height of the cone and the altitude of it are same.

(c) Given an oblique cylinder, its axis and its altitude are not congruent.

111. Suppose we cut the following solid of revolution by a plane that contains the axis of rotation. Find the area of the planar figure.

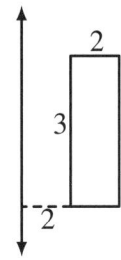

112. If the area of a great circle of the sphere is 9π, find the surface area of the sphere.

113. David bought a triangular prism. The bases are equilateral triangle with side lengths 4 units. If the height of the prism is 5 units, find the surface area of David's prism.

114. Find the volume of the following regular hexagonal prism whose base length is 6 and the slant height is $12\sqrt{2}$. (One must assume that the altitude of the figure shown as a dotted segment is perpendicular to the base.)

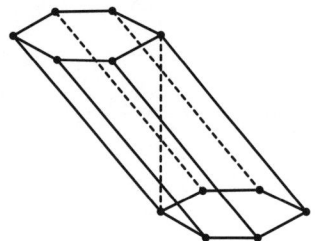

115. If a sphere whose radius is 1 fits inside the cylinder, find the volume ratio of a sphere to cylinder.

Skill Practice

Problem 1
How many regular polyhedra have their faces triangle?

Problem 2
How many faces does a cube have?

Problem 3
Find the surface area of a cuboid whose dimension is given by $3 \times 4 \times 5$.

Problem 4
How many vertices does a regular dodecahedron have?

Problem 5
Find the volume of a semisphere whose radius is 3.

Problem 6
Find the volume of a regular tetrahedron if the side length is 6.

Problem 7
Find the volume of a right triangular prism if the base is an isosceles triangle whose legs are of length 6 and the height of the solid is 5.

Problem 8
Find the surface area of hemisphere if its radius is 4.

Problem 9
A right circular cone has its base radius 3 and its height 4. Find the lateral surface area.

Problem 10
A rhombicuboctahedron has 8 equilateral triangle faces and 18 square faces. If there are 24 vertices, how many edges are there?

Answer Key

1. 3

2. 6

3. 94

4. 20

5. 18π

6. $18\sqrt{2}$

7. 90

8. 48π

9. 15π

10. 48

Topic 12
Trigonometric Ratio

12.1 Basic Ratio 216

12.1 Basic Ratio

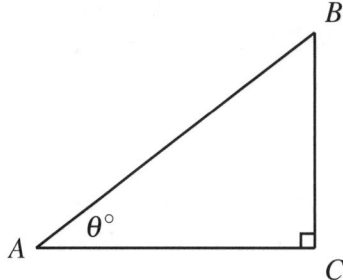

Given a right triangle ABC and an angle θ, there are six trigonometric ratios.

- Sine : the ratio of opposite to hypotenuse, i.e., $\sin\theta = \dfrac{a}{c}$.

- Cosine : the ratio of adjacent to hypotenuse, i.e., $\cos\theta = \dfrac{b}{c}$.

- Tangent : the ratio of opposite to adjacent, i.e., $\tan\theta = \dfrac{a}{b}$.

- Cosecant : the reciprocal of sine, i.e., $\csc\theta = \dfrac{1}{\sin\theta}$.

- Secant : the reciprocal of cosine, i.e., $\sec\theta = \dfrac{1}{\cos\theta}$.

- Cotangent : the reciprocal of tangent, i.e., $\cot\theta = \dfrac{1}{\tan\theta}$.

There are special right triangles that will appear in Trigonometry. Two special triangles, $30° - 60° - 90°$ and $45° - 45° - 90°$, result in trigonometric ratios. Other than tangent values, sine value and cosine value are either $1/2$, $\sqrt{2}/2$, or $\sqrt{3}/2$. Notice that $\cos(45°)$ or $\sin(45°)$ are $1/\sqrt{2}$. If the denominator is rationalized, then the ratio turns into $\sqrt{2}/2$.

Now, let's extend trigonometric ratio into more than acute angles. There are two things to check. First is the base angle(or reference angle), and the second is C.A.S.T sign rule.

Reference angle is an acute angle formed between the x-axis and the rotated ray. For instance, were $\sin(120°)$ to be computed, we use the fact that $60°$ is the reference angle. What we know from reference angle is that $|\sin(120°)| = |\sin(60°)|$. All we have to know is the sign of $\sin(120°)$, determined by C.A.S.T rule.

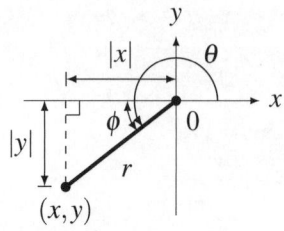

Try to compute $\cos(120°)$ using both reference angle and C.A.S.T rule. Its absolute value must be equal to $\cos(60°)$, while its sign is negative.

Reference angle is formed when we draw a perpendicular line segment from the point to the *x*-axis. Let's practice with more examples.

Example 95

Determine the exact value of $\sin(30°) + \cos(45°)$.

Example 96

Evaluate the exact value of the following expressions.

(a) $\sin(120°)$

(b) $\cos(135°)$

(c) $\tan(225°)$

(d) $\cos(315°)$

(e) $\sin(330°)$

Here is the solution to the examples covered in the previous page.

Example 95. $\sin(30°) + \cos(45°) = \dfrac{1}{2} + \dfrac{\sqrt{2}}{2} = \dfrac{1+\sqrt{2}}{2}$.

Example 96.

(a) $\sin(120°) = \sin(60°) = \dfrac{\sqrt{3}}{2}$.

(b) $\cos(135°) = -\cos(45°) = -\dfrac{\sqrt{2}}{2}$.

(c) $\tan(225°) = \tan(45°) = 1$.

(d) $\cos(315°) = \cos(45°) = \dfrac{\sqrt{2}}{2}$.

(e) $\sin(330°) = -\sin(30°) = -\dfrac{1}{2}$.

HISTORICAL FACT

The history of sine, cosine, and tangent reflects centuries of mathematical evolution, spanning multiple cultures. Originating in ancient India, trigonometric ideas were formalized by scholars like Aryabhata and Brahmagupta, who introduced concepts such as the half-chord, now recognized as the sine function. The Sanskrit word jya (chord) later evolved through Arabic translations as jiba, misinterpreted in Latin as sinus, giving rise to the modern term sine.

In the Islamic Golden Age, mathematicians like Al-Khwarizmi and Al-Battani refined trigonometry, using it in astronomy and navigation. They defined ratios for angles and created comprehensive trigonometric tables. Their work significantly influenced European mathematicians during the Renaissance.

The tangent and cosine functions gained prominence in the 17th century with the work of European mathematicians like Isaac Newton and Leonard Euler, who formalized trigonometric functions in calculus. From calculating planetary motions to engineering marvels, these functions have become foundational tools in mathematics, uniting ancient discoveries with modern advancements.

Walk-Through Practices

116. Given $\theta = 30°, 45°, 60°$, evaluate the following trigonometric ratio: $\sin(\theta)$, $\cos(\theta)$, $\tan(\theta)$, $\csc(\theta)$, $\sec(\theta)$ and $\cot(\theta)$.

117. (a) If $\tan(\theta) = 1$ for acute angle θ, find $\cos(\theta)$ and $\sin(\theta)$.

(b) If $\tan(\phi) = 3$, find $\cos(\phi)$ and $\sin(\phi)$ for an acute angle ϕ.

118. If $0° < \theta < 360°$, and θ has the reference angle (or base angle) of $45°$, find θ if

(a) it is in the 2nd quadrant.

(b) it is in the 3rd quadrant.

(c) it is in the 4th quadrant.

119. Without using a calculator, evaluate

(a) $\dfrac{\cos(135°)}{\sin(120°) + \cos(150°)}$

(b) $\dfrac{\sin(27°)}{\cos(63°)}$

120. If $\sin(\theta) = \dfrac{1}{2}$ for acute angle θ, find the value of $\cos(90° - \theta)\sin(\theta)$.

Solutions to walk-through practices can be found in the solution manual. Go to page 225.

Skill Practice

Problem 1
Find the exact value of $\sin(60°)$.

Problem 2
Find the exact value of $\cos(45°)$.

Problem 3
Find the exact value of $\tan(30°)$.

Problem 4
Find the exact value of $\sin(150°)$.

Problem 5
Find the exact value of $\cos(300°)$.

Problem 6
Evaluate $\sin^2(30°) + \cos^2(30°)$.

Problem 7
Evaluate $1 + \tan^2(45°)$.

Problem 8
Evaluate $1 + \cot^2(30°)$.

Problem 9
Find the exact value of $\cos(36°)$.

Problem 10
Find the exact value of $\sin(54°)$.

Answer Key

1. $\dfrac{\sqrt{3}}{2}$

2. $\dfrac{\sqrt{2}}{2}$

3. $\dfrac{\sqrt{3}}{3}$

4. $\dfrac{1}{2}$

5. $\dfrac{1}{2}$

6. 1

7. 2

8. 4

9. $\dfrac{1+\sqrt{5}}{4}$

10. $\dfrac{1+\sqrt{5}}{4}$

BEFORE YOU MOVE ON

François Viète and the Origins of Trigonometry

Introduction: François Viète (1540-1603), also known as Franciscus Vieta, was a French mathematician who played a crucial role in the development of modern algebra and trigonometry. Often regarded as the "Father of Modern Algebraic Notation," Viète made significant contributions to trigonometry by introducing algebraic methods to solve trigonometric problems.

Contributions to Trigonometry:

- *Trigonometric Identities:* Viète established algebraic formulas for trigonometric functions, laying the groundwork for modern trigonometric analysis.

- *Angle Addition Formulas:* He derived the famous angle addition and subtraction identities:

$$\sin(a \pm b) = \sin a \cos b \pm \cos a \sin b, \quad \cos(a \pm b) = \cos a \cos b \mp \sin a \sin b.$$

- *Algebraic Approach:* By representing trigonometric relationships algebraically, he unified the fields of algebra and trigonometry.

The Viète Formula: One of his most notable contributions is the infinite product representation of π, known as the Viète formula:

$$\frac{2}{\pi} = \prod_{n=1}^{\infty} \cos\left(\frac{\pi}{2^{n+1}}\right).$$

This formula linked trigonometry and infinite series, highlighting Viète's innovative approach to mathematics.

Historical Note: Viète lived during the Renaissance, a time of rapid scientific and mathematical advancements. His work bridged ancient Greek trigonometry and modern mathematical practices, earning him a place as one of the great pioneers in the history of mathematics.

Solution to 120 Walk-Through Exercises

1. This is a combination of counting in geometrical context. There are $\frac{4 \times 3}{2} = 6$ lines.

2. The first segment should be labeled as $\overline{AB}$ or $\overline{BA}$ with overline symbol. The second line is either $\overleftrightarrow{CD}$ or $\overleftrightarrow{DC}$ with overline arrows that go both left and right. The third ray is $\overrightarrow{EF}$ with one arrow that goes right.

3. Since $3x - 3 = 12 - 2x$, we get $5x = 15$, so $x = 3$. Therefore, $3(3) - 3 = 9 - 3 = 6$ is the length we want.

4. Let the distance between $(4, 11)$ and $(-2, 3)$ be x. Then, $x^2 = (4-(-2))^2 + (11-3)^2 = 10^2$, so $x = 10$.

5. The x-coordinate of the point W is $\frac{1}{3} \times (-5) + \frac{2}{3} \times 3 = \frac{1}{3}$, and the y-coordinate of W is $\frac{1}{3} \times (-12) + \frac{2}{3} \times 8 = \frac{4}{3}$, so $\left(\frac{1}{3}, \frac{4}{3}\right)$.

6. Since $m\angle AOC = 90°$, we get $3x - 10 + x = 90°$, so $4x = 100°$. Therefore, $x = 25°$.

7. (a) Angles are adjacent and complementary. (b) Angles are adjacent but not necessarily *supplementary*. (c) Since we do not know whether it is right angle, we only know they are *adjacent*.

8. (a) A is on the line l. (b) B, C, D are not on the line l.

9. (a) Line $\overleftrightarrow{AD}$ is parallel to line $\overleftrightarrow{BC}$. (b) Lines $\overleftrightarrow{AD}$, $\overleftrightarrow{BC}$, and $\overleftrightarrow{DC}$ also satisfy this condition.

10. Like exercise 1, this is a counting question in geometrical context. We have $\frac{4 \times 3 \times 2}{6} = 4$ planes formed.

11. (a) There are three lines parallel to line $\overleftrightarrow{AB}$: lines $\overleftrightarrow{CD}$, $\overleftrightarrow{EF}$, and $\overleftrightarrow{HG}$. (b) There are four skew lines to line $\overleftrightarrow{BC}$: lines $\overleftrightarrow{EF}$, $\overleftrightarrow{HG}$, $\overleftrightarrow{AE}$, and $\overleftrightarrow{DH}$.

12. There are three edges AD, BF, and CE perpendicular to the plane ABC.

13. Other than a pair formed by faces ABC and DFE, any pair of other faces is not parallel to each other.

14. First, for conjunction, we write $5+(-5)=0$, and natural numbers are all even. On the other hand, for disjunction, we write $5+(-5)=0$ or natural numbers are all even.

15. For $\neg p$, it is F, F, T, T, respectively. Likewise, for $\neg p \cup q$, it is T, F, T, T, respectively.

16. (a) The statement is true. (b) The statement is false. (c) The statement is true. (d) The statement is true.

17. The converse is false because two skew lines on a space do not meet but they are not parallel.

18. (a) This is not valid. (b) It is valid by the law of detachment.

19. (1) Reflexive : Use definition of congruent segments. (2) Symmetric : Use definition of congruent segments, symmetric property, and definition of congruent segments, again. (3) Transitive : Use definition of congruent segments, transitive property, and definition of congruent segments, again.

20. $3(x-2)=6 \implies \dfrac{3(x-2)}{3}=\dfrac{6}{3} \implies x-2=2 \implies x-2+2=2+2 \implies x+0=4 \implies x=4$

21. Since A, B, C are collinear, $AC = AB + BC$. Then,
$AC - BC = AB + BC - BC = AB + 0 = AB$. Therefore, $AB = AC - BC$ by segment addition postulate.

22. If $AB = AC$ and $AB = 4$, then $AC = 4$, by transitive property.

23. Let $\angle A$ and $\angle B$ form a linear pair. Then, they form a straight angle. Therefore,, $m\angle A + m\angle B = 180°$. They are supplementary by definition.

24. Let $\angle X$ and $\angle Y$ form a right angle, denoted by $\angle C$ in the problem. Then, $m\angle X + m\angle Y = 90°$. They are complementary by definition.

25. $m\angle A + m\angle B = 180°$ and $m\angle C + m\angle B = 180°$, as given. By transitive property, $m\angle A + m\angle B = m\angle C + m\angle B$. By translation property, $m\angle A = m\angle C$. By definition of congruent angles, $\angle A \cong \angle C$.

26. $m\angle A + m\angle B = 90°$ and $m\angle C + m\angle B = 90°$, as given. By transitive property, $m\angle A + m\angle B = m\angle C + m\angle B$. By translation property, $m\angle A = m\angle C$. By definition of angle congruence, $\angle A \cong \angle C$.

27. $\angle 1$ and $\angle 2$ are linear pair, so $m\angle 1 + m\angle 2 = 180°$. Also, $\angle 2$ and $\angle 3$ are linear pair, so $m\angle 2 + m\angle 3 = 180°$. Hence, by walk-through 25, $m\angle 1 = m\angle 3$, so $\angle 1 \cong \angle 3$.

28. First apply the definition of perpendicular lines and right angles. Then, using the definition of linear pair and substitution, find the measure of $\angle Y$, denoted in the problem. Use vertical angle postulate and transitive property, conclude that all angles are right, by the definition of right angles.

29. Apply the definition of right angles and transitive property, conclude all right angles are congruent, according to the definition of congruent angles.

30. This is corollary of walk-through 28.

31. Let the two angles be $\angle X$ and $\angle Y$. Since they are congruent, $m\angle X = m\angle Y$. According to the definition of supplementary angles, $m\angle X + m\angle Y = 180°$. By substitution, $2m\angle X = 180°$. By translation, $m\angle X = 90°$. By transitive property, $m\angle Y = 90°$. By definition, they are both right angles.

32. Let the two angles be $\angle X$ and $\angle Y$. It is given that $\angle X$ and $\angle Y$ form a linear pair. Hence by the definition of linear pair, they are supplementary. Repeat the same process as in the walk-through 23. Then, similar to what walk-through 31 addresses, we get right angles for $\angle X$ and $\angle Y$.

33. $(\angle 1, \angle 5)$, $(\angle 2, \angle 6)$, $(\angle 3, \angle 7)$, and $(\angle 4, \angle 8)$ are corresponding angles. $(\angle 4, \angle 6)$ and $(\angle 3, \angle 5)$ are alternate interior angles. Also, $(\angle 2, \angle 8)$ and $(\angle 1, \angle 7)$ are alternate exterior angles. Consecutive exterior angles are $(\angle 1, \angle 8)$ and $(\angle 2, \angle 7)$. There are four pairs for

vertical angle pairs, i.e., (∠1,∠3), (∠2,∠4), (∠5,∠7), and (∠6,∠8). Lastly, consecutive interior angles are (∠4,∠5) and (∠3,∠6).

34. Apply vertical angle postulate and corresponding angle postulate.

35. Let consecutive interior angles be ∠B and ∠C. Let ∠A be the corresponding angle of one of the two given angles, without loss of generality. Then, ∠A ≅ ∠D. Since ∠C and ∠D form a linear pair, ∠C and ∠D are supplementary. Hence,
$m\angle C + m\angle D = m\angle C + m\angle A = m\angle C + m\angle B = 180°$, so ∠B and ∠C are supplementary.

36. Let alternate exterior angles be ∠A and ∠C. Let ∠B be the corresponding angle of ∠A. Then, ∠A ≅ ∠B by corresponding angle postulate. Then, ∠B ≅ ∠C by vertical angle postulate. Hence, ∠A ≅ ∠C by transitive property of congruence.

37. According to the definition of perpendicular lines, the definition of right angles, the corresponding angle postulate, and transitive property, we conclude that l is perpendicular to the transversal, according to the definition of perpendicular lines.

38. By drawing a parallel auxiliary line, we get $x = 70° + 45° = 115°$ by corresponding angle postulate, alternate interior angle theorem, and angle addition postulate.

39. Since it is parallel, we have the slope value of 3. Since it passes through $(-3, -5)$, we get $y = 3x + b$ where $-5 = 3(-3) + b$. Hence, $b = 4$, so $y = 3x + 4$.

40. If we change $4x + 8y = 12$ into $8y = -4x + 12$, then $y = -\frac{1}{2}x + \frac{3}{2}$. Hence, the slope is given by $-\frac{1}{2}$. Therefore, the perpendicular line has a slope of a negative reciprocal of $-\frac{1}{2}$, which is equal to 2.

41. Apply the original condition, vertical angle postulate, and the converse of corresponding angle postulate to show that lines l and m are parallel.

42. Apply the definition of supplementary angles, the definition of linear pair. In the middle, one must apply transitive property and translation property to show that corresponding angles are congruent. Hence, apply the converse of corresponding angle postulate to show that l and m are parallel.

43. Apply the definition of congruent angles, vertical angle postulate, and transitive property show that corresponding angles are congruent. Hence, apply the converse of corresponding angle postulate to conclude that l and m are parallel.

44. Assume that two lines are perpendicular to the given transversal. Then, each of the two lines form $90°$ to the transversal. Then, corresponding angles are congruent to $90°$, so the two lines are parallel, according to the converse of corresponding angle postulate.

45. (a) Use the linear distance notion to get the distance of 2 units. (b) Use the quadratic distance formula to get $\sqrt{(3-2)^2 + (1-2)^2} = \sqrt{2}$ unit.

46. First, find the perpendicular transversal to the both line, $y = -\frac{1}{2}x$. Then, we find out that $\left(-\frac{4}{5}, \frac{2}{5}\right)$ is the point of intersection between $y = -\frac{1}{2}x$ and $y = 2x + 2$. Hence, the distance between $(0,0)$ and $\left(-\frac{4}{5}, \frac{2}{5}\right)$ is equal to $\sqrt{\frac{20}{25}} = \frac{\sqrt{20}}{5} = \frac{2\sqrt{5}}{5}$.

47. $AB = \sqrt{2^2 + 1^2} = \sqrt{5}$, $BC = \sqrt{1^2 + 3^2} = \sqrt{10}$ and $CA = \sqrt{1^2 + 2^2} = \sqrt{5}$. Hence, $\triangle ABC$ is a right isosceles triangle.

48. Apply A.I.A Theorem to show that $\angle A \cong \angle D$ and $\angle C \cong \angle E$. Then, use definition of congruent angles to show that their measures are equal. Since $m\angle D + m\angle B + m\angle E = 180°$ is given, apply substitution property to show that $m\angle A + m\angle B + m\angle C = 180°$.

49. Apply A.I.A Theorem to show that $\angle D \cong \angle A$. Then, the definition of congruent angles states that $m\angle D = m\angle A$. It is easy to see that A.I.A Theorem also states that $m\angle D + m\angle B = m\angle E$. Substitution property shows that $m\angle A + m\angle B = m\angle E$.

50. $40°$

51. Use CPCTC and use the transitive property of congruence. Since $\angle A \cong \angle D, \angle D \cong \angle X$, then $\angle A \cong \angle X$. Likewise, we get $\angle B \cong \angle Y$ and $\angle C \cong \angle Z$. Now, since $\overline{AB} \cong \overline{DE}, \overline{DE} \cong \overline{XY}$, we get $\overline{AB} \cong \overline{XY}$. Likewise, we get $\overline{BC} \cong \overline{YZ}$ and $\overline{CA} \cong \overline{ZX}$. Therefore, two triangles $\triangle ABC$ and $\triangle XYZ$ are congruent.

52. No, they are not congruent since $AB \neq DE, BC \neq EF, CA \neq FD$. None of the triangle congruences, SSS, SAS, or ASA, can be applied.

53. Given a right triangle, we call the longest side as hypotenuse while the others are called legs. Let's label two right triangles $\triangle ABC$ and $\triangle DEF$. Since $AB^2 + BC^2 = AC^2$ and $DE^2 + EF^2 = DF^2$, while $AB = DE$ and $AC = DF$, then the other sides are automatically congruent, i.e., $BC = EF$. Therefore, we can use SSS congruence. It is important to mark that SAS congruence postulate can also be applied.

54. Since two angles are given, the other angle can be found by S.I.A.T theorem. Notice that the angle measures of the remaining angle for each triangle are equal. Therefore, apply ASA congruent postulate to show that the triangles are congruent.

55. Let's label two given triangles as $\triangle ABC$ and $\triangle DEF$ where $\angle B$ and $\angle E$ are right angles. Then, the given assumption tells us that $\angle A \cong \angle D$, $\overline{AB} \cong \overline{DE}$, and $\angle B \cong \angle E$ by right angle, so we get two congruent triangles by ASA congruence postulate.

56. Since two legs are congruent to the corresponding two legs. We have two sides are equal. The right angles are included in the legs, so the two triangles are congruent by SAS congruence postulate. Or, one may apply Pythagorean Theorem to show that two triangles are congruent by SSS congruence postulate.

57. Call two triangles $\triangle ABC$ and $\triangle DEF$ where $\angle B$ and $\angle E$ are right angles. We can use AAS congruence theorem directly to the given triangles. On the other hand, get the measure of remaining angle by S.I.A.T theorem to use ASA congruence postulate.

58. First, $\angle CDF \cong \angle EDF$, by the definition of angle bisector. Also, $\angle CFD$ and $\angle EFD$ are right angles, by the definition of perpendicular lines. Now, look at $\overline{DF}$, which is common to $\triangle DFC$ and $\triangle EDF$. Since $\overline{DF} \cong \overline{DF}$ by reflexive property, apply ASA congruence postulate to show that two triangles are congruent.

59. Let's start with a triangle ABC with $AB = AC$. Let D be the point on $\overline{BC}$ such that $\overline{AD}$ is perpendicular to $\overline{BC}$. By assumption, $AB = AC$ and $AD = AD$, so apply HL congruence theorem and CPCTC to conclude that $\angle B \cong \angle C$. This proves IT Theorem.

60. Let's start with a triangle ABC where $\angle B$ and $\angle C$ are congruent by assumption. Then, let D be the intersection point between the perpendicular bisector of $\angle BAC$ and $\overline{BC}$. Then, $\triangle ABD$

and $\triangle ACD$ are congruent by AL congruence theorem. Therefore, $AB = AC$ by CPCTC. This proves the converse of IT Theorem.

61. $60°$

62. 10

63. $36°$

64. 30 unit^2

65. 19, where all side lengths satisfy triangular inequality.

66. $\dfrac{10}{\sqrt{3}} \left(= \dfrac{10\sqrt{3}}{3} \right)$

67. $r = 2$

68. Assume that $AX = BY$. Let G be the centroid. Since $AG = \dfrac{2}{3}AX$ and $BG = \dfrac{2}{3}BY$, we get $AG = BG$, so $\triangle ABG$ is an isosceles triangle. Then, $\angle GAB \cong \angle GBA$, so we apply SAS congruence postulate to $\triangle ABY$ and $\triangle BAX$. Therefore, $AY = BX$ by CPCTC. Since X and Y are respective midpoints according to the definition of median, $AY = YC$ and $BX = XC$. Therefore, $AC = BC$ by substitution and translation property.

69. $45°$

70. $\dfrac{169}{24}$

71. 3cm

72. $9\sqrt{3}$

73. $\dfrac{225(\sqrt{3}+1)}{2}$

74. Since $AB = AC < BC$, then $m\angle C = m\angle B < m\angle A$, according to Angle-Side Theorem (or Side-Angle Theorem). Therefore, $m\angle A + m\angle B + m\angle C < m\angle A + m\angle A + m\angle A = 3m\angle A$. Hence, $180° < 3m\angle A$, so $60° < m\angle A$.

75. There are three triangle triples, i.e., $(3,8,9)$, $(4,7,9)$ and $(5,6,9)$.

76. By side length condition, $1 \leq x$. On the other hand, by triangular inequality, $x < 4$. Therefore, $x = 1, 2, 3$. There are three possible values of x.

77. $\dfrac{50}{3}$

78. $QA = \dfrac{9}{2}$

79. $CE = 2$

80. $\dfrac{15}{2}$

81. Since the length ratio is $1:2$, the area ratio is $1:4$. Therefore, the small triangle CDF has the area of 6 square units.

82. If you draw one diagonal, then there are two adjacent triangles. Since each of the triangle

has the sum of interior angles equal to 180°, we get 360°. The sum of exterior angles is 360° for a convex n-gon, and it is true for $n = 4$.

83. Given a trapezoid $ABCD$, let E and F be the midpoint of $\overline{AB}$ and $\overline{CD}$, respectively. If we extend $\overline{AF}$ to get the intersection point between the extended line $\overline{BC}$ and $\overline{AF}$ as G. Then, $\triangle ADF \cong \triangle GCF$ by ASA congruence. Also, $EF : BG = 1 : 2$ by similar triangles. Since $BG = BC + CG$, we get $EF : BC + CG = EF : BC + AD = 1 : 2$. Therefore, the midsegment is the average of the bases of the trapezoid.

84. Let $ABCD$ be a parallelogram. Let E be the point of intersection between the diagonals $\overline{AC}$ and $\overline{BD}$. It is true $\overline{AD} \cong \overline{CB}$, $\angle CAD \cong \angle ACB$, and $\angle ADB \cong \angle DBC$. Hence, $\triangle ADE \cong \triangle CBE$, thus the diagonals are bisected at E by CPCTC.

85. Since diagonals are bisected, we get four congruent right triangles whose length of legs is 3 and 4. Hence, the hypotenuse length is 5. The perimeter is 20. On the other hand, the area of the rhombus is $4(6) = 24$.

86. Since we want to show that $EFGH$ is a rectangle, we look for a way to find the measures of each angle of $EFGH$. Now, E, F, G, H are the midpoints of $ABCD$ where $ABCD$ is a rhombus. Hence, we find out that the vertices of $EFGH$ divide the sides of $ABCD$ into eight equal segments. Since $ABCD$ is also parallelogram, $\angle A = \angle C$ and $\angle B = \angle D$. Therefore, $\triangle AEH \cong \triangle CGF$ and $\triangle BEF \cong \triangle DGH$. It is obvious that each of these small triangles is isosceles, so we can let $\angle AEH = a$ and $\angle DGH = b$ and identify equal angles as shown. Finally, we see that each angle of $EFGH$ has measure $180° - a - b$. Thus, all the angles of $EFGH$ are equal and $EFGH$ must be a rectangle by definition.

87. 2

88. Since $\dfrac{180°(n-2)}{n} = 168°$, $n = 30$. Therefore we get a 30-gon.

89. $1 : \sqrt{2}$

90. $1 : 24$

91. $1 : 2$

234   The Essential Guide to Geometry

92. $\sqrt{3}:2$

93. For the first vertex, there are n choices to make. For the second vertex, we cannot choose two adjacent vertices, so we have $n-3$ points to choose. We need to divide $n(n-3)$ by 2 because we do not want order between the two vertices.

94. It is 13-gon, so we get $\dfrac{13 \times 10}{2} = 65$ possible diagonals formed by connecting any pair of two vertices.

95. Call $m\angle AOB = x$, then $\angle BOC = 180° - 2x$. Therefore, $m\angle CBO = x$. Hence, by the converse of alternate interior angle theorem, $\overline{BC}$ is parallel to $\overline{AD}$.

96. $x = 40°$ and $y = 140°$

97. By similar triangles, we get the ratio $AC : BC = EC : DC$. Let AC be x. Therefore, $x : 3 = 5 : 4$, so $x = \dfrac{15}{4}$.

98. $2\sqrt{3}$

99. $35°$

100. $35°$

101. It might take some time to see $\triangle ABP \sim \triangle ADB$ by AA similarity, i.e., $\angle B \cong \angle C$ by isosceles triangle and $\angle C \cong \angle D$ by common intercepted arc. Hence, $AB : AP = AD : AB$, so $AB^2 = (AP)(AD)$.

102. $A' = (-1,-1), B' = (2,0), C' = (1,-3)$.

103. E

104. Yes, it also coincides with the original figure because $35° \times 11 = 385° = 360° + 25°$.

105. Regular hexagon.

106. $3\sqrt{5}$

107. The shortest path is a path that has the length of $\sqrt{16+49} = \sqrt{65}$ miles.

108. It is a triangle formed by the new vertices $A'(-3,4), B'(-2,4), C'(-2,2)$.

109. It is a dodecahedron.

110. (a) False. Think about an oblique cylinder. (b) False. The altitude is the segment, while the height is its length. (c) True.

111. There are 2 right triangles in the slice. Hence, we get 12.

112. We need four great circles to cover the sphere, hence, it is 36π

113. First, let's compute the area of the bases. There are two equilateral triangles with the base length of 4. Hence, $4 \times 2\sqrt{3} \times \dfrac{1}{2} = 4\sqrt{3}$ is the area of one triangle. There are two of these so we have $8\sqrt{3}$ for the triangle bases. Second, the lateral faces are rectangles and there are three congruent rectangles, each of which has the area of $4 \times 5 = 20$. Therefore, the total surface area is $8\sqrt{3} + 60$ square units.

114. The base area is given by $9\sqrt{3} \times 6 = 54\sqrt{3}$. Since the height is 12, we get the volume of this solid as $648\sqrt{3}$ cubic units.

115. Let's compute the volume of the sphere, which is given by $\dfrac{4}{3}\pi(1)^3$. On the other hand, the volume of the cylinder is given by $\pi(1)^2 \times 2$, because the sphere diameter is the height of the cylinder. Hence, the ratio is equal to $2 : 3$.

116. $\sin(30°) = \cos(60°) = \dfrac{1}{2}$, and $\sin(60°) = \cos(30°) = \dfrac{\sqrt{3}}{2}$, and

236   The Essential Guide to Geometry

$\sin(45°) = \cos(45°) = \dfrac{\sqrt{2}}{2}$. Hence, $\csc(30°) = \sec(60°) = 2$, and $\csc(60°) = \sec(30°) = \dfrac{2}{\sqrt{3}} = \dfrac{2\sqrt{3}}{3}$, and $\csc(45°) = \sec(45°) = \dfrac{2}{\sqrt{2}} = \sqrt{2}$. Finally, $\tan(30°) = \cot(60°) = \dfrac{1}{\sqrt{3}} = \dfrac{\sqrt{3}}{3}$, and $\tan(60°) = \cot(30°) = \sqrt{3}$, and $\tan(45°) = \cot(45°) = 1$.

117. (a) $\cos(\theta) = \sin(\theta) = \dfrac{1}{\sqrt{2}} = \dfrac{\sqrt{2}}{2}$. (b) $\cos(\phi) = \dfrac{1}{\sqrt{10}} = \dfrac{\sqrt{10}}{10}$ and $\sin(\phi) = \dfrac{3}{\sqrt{10}} = \dfrac{3\sqrt{10}}{10}$.

118. (a) 135° (b) 225° (c) 315°

119. (a) Since $\cos(135°) = -\cos(45°) = -\dfrac{\sqrt{2}}{2}$, $\sin(120°) = \sin(60°) = \dfrac{\sqrt{3}}{2}$, and $\cos(150°) = -\cos(30°) = -\dfrac{\sqrt{3}}{2}$, the denominator turns into 0. Hence, it is undefined. (b) By drawing an associated triangle, we find out that $\sin(27°) = \cos(63°)$, although we cannot compute exact value without a calculator. Hence, $\dfrac{\sin(27°)}{\cos(63°)} = 1$.

120. First, θ is acute, so $90° - \theta$ is also acute. Hence, $\cos(90° - \theta)$ is positive and $\sin(\theta)$ is assumed to be positive. Also, $\cos(90° - \theta) = \sin(\theta)$, which we can check by drawing an associated triangle. Therefore, we get $(\sin(\theta))^2 = \sin^2(\theta) = \dfrac{1}{4}$.

MEMO

MEMO